EMPLOYMENT DISCRIMINATION

The material in this book is based on research prepared for the Employment and Training Administration, U.S. Department of Labor (Grant no. 21-48-74-03) under authority of Section 311 of the Comprehensive Employment and Training Act of 1973, as amended. Researchers undertaking such projects under government sponsorship are encouraged to express freely their professional judgment. Therefore, points of view or opinions stated in this document do not necessarily represent the official position or policy of the Department of Labor. Reproduction, in whole or in part, is permitted for any purpose of the U.S. government.

EMPLOYMENT DISCRIMINATION:

The Impact of Legal and Administrative Remedies

Ray Marshall

Charles B. Knapp

Malcolm H. Liggett

Robert W. Glover

PRAEGER PUBLISHERS
Praeger Special Studies

New York   •   London   •   Sydney   •   Toronto

0764913   ~~44592~~

Library of Congress Cataloging in Publication Data
Main entry under title:

Employment discrimination.

 1. Discrimination in employment--Law and legis-
lation--United States. I. Marshall, F. Ray.
KF3464.E45   344'.73'01133   78-17333
ISBN 0-03-045356-9

PRAEGER PUBLISHERS
PRAEGER SPECIAL STUDIES
383 Madison Avenue, New York, N.Y. 10017, U.S.A.

Published in the United States of America in 1978
by Praeger Publishers,
A Division of Holt, Rinehart and Winston, CBS, Inc.

89   038   987654321

Printed in the United States of America

PREFACE

This book was written when I was conducting research in the field of employment discrimination while I was Director of the Center for the Study of Human Resources. Since becoming Secretary of Labor, I have found that my earlier views on employment discrimination have generally been reinforced. I continue to believe that the most effective way to combat employment discrimination is to encourage employers and unions to voluntarily undertake remedial measures. Steps devised and undertaken by employers, unions, and minorities themselves are likely to be far more effective than orders imposed on them by government. However, public policy—including the use of laws and regulations—is often required to stimulate those who resist changing employment practices to take measures to achieve equal opportunity. Public policy also helps establish a supportive environment in which well-intentioned employers and union leaders can take remedial steps with less fear of retaliation by workers, other employers, or consumers.

Circumstances may demand, at times, that government establish goals and timetables which impose upon employers the obligation of making a good faith effort to achieve specified standards of performance. There are important, often overlooked, distinctions between goals and quotas. For example, achievement of a prescribed number is the sole basis for judging performance under a quota, while evidence of good faith efforts is the criteria under goals and timetables.

Overall, there has been a healthy maturing of procedures in equal opportunity enforcement. Initial efforts focused largely on overt discrimination and were directed at identifying and prosecuting individual discriminators. Proceedings were often charged with high emotion and were strongly confrontative in nature. With time, efforts shifted to combatting institutional discrimination. This development is helpful. It de-escalates emotionalism and shifts emphasis from proving guilt to using reason to devise effective remedies for discriminatory employment patterns which may be the result of no one individual. Given the proper circumstances and good faith on the part of the parties involved, it provides a better opportunity for working together toward a remedy.

Attempts to achieve equal opportunity by reducing job-related standards or creating different standards based on race or sex are doomed to fail. Such policy lowers productivity, invites the backlash of fellow workers, creates problems for managers, harms the consuming public, and debases the individuals it is designed to serve. The application of different standards can impose a severe psychological burden on monorities and women. The message of these standards is clear—we don't think you are good enough to meet *our* standards.

While I do not believe in special standards for minorities or women, I do believe there are special things that can be done to help minorities and women

v

meet legitimate standards. It seems entirely reasonable that the history of discrimination among certain employers may make minorities and women wary of applying after the organization has embraced integration. It is clear that special recruiting, supportive, and remedial programs for minorities and women who need them can make an important contribution to equal opportunity. Organizations for minorities and women play a key role in developing and implementing these programs.

We have made great strides in recent years in the battle against employment discrimination. But most of our efforts have focused on the demand side of the equation. That is, we have been concerned almost exclusively with ways to get employers to embrace equal opportunity.

This is clearly of paramount importance. But there is another side of the equation—the supply side. Unless we have a sufficient stream of minorities and women with qualifications and training to fill available vacancies, we are severely limited in what we can do to integrate employment. Clearly, education and training will have to be better related to work.

Employment discrimination is an area which calls for further policy-oriented research. We need better understanding of the dynamics of employment discrimination, how to remedy it, and how to prevent it. Such research is not likely to spring from the narrow perspectives of any one academic discipline. Nor is it likely to come from concentration on any one group, such as employers. Rather, it will develop from a systematic overview of all the actors and environmental factors involved in employment discrimination.

The pursuit of equal employment opportunity in the United States is irreversible. No court decision or public policy action can turn back the tide. Achievement in this public policy arena brings greater demands for full realization of equal opportunity. Lack of achievement mobilizes change even more. Much has been accomplished since the first executive order was issued by President Franklin Roosevelt in 1941; yet much remains to be done.

Ray Marshall

ACKNOWLEDGMENTS

This report represents the cooperative efforts of several people. Most of the field work in construction was performed by Charles Knapp, and he is the primary author of Chapter 2. Malcolm Liggett conducted the field work on shipbuilding and authored Chapter 3. The introduction and summary and conclusions were written primarily by Ray Marshall and Robert Glover. It should be noted that this report also draws on research on the steel and paper industries as well as previous work by the authors on the topic of equal employment opportunity.

We wish to acknowledge our debt to the hundreds of persons who took time from their busy schedules to interview with us and to provide information for this study. They included workers, compliance officials, union representatives, employers, minority participants, and attorneys. Although the numbers are too great to permit individual mention, we express our gratitude and our hope that the final product brings a new understanding of discrimination and ways to combat it.

In addition, we wish to thank Charles Loring, who conducted research on the steel industry. Also appreciated are the encouragement and guidance of Dr. Howard Rosen and Ellen Sehgal of the Office of Research and Development, U.S. Department of Labor. Finally, we thank Jane Tonn, Kyna Simmons, Sandy Olmstead, and Susie Turner for their care and diligence in typing the various drafts of this report.

Of course, the reader is reminded that the authors alone remain responsible for the content and conclusions of this report.

CONTENTS

Page

PREFACE by Ray Marshall   v

ACKNOWLEDGMENTS   vii

LIST OF TABLES AND FIGURE   viii

LIST OF ACRONYMS   xvii

GLOSSARY OF TERMS   xix

Chapter

1   INTRODUCTION   1

    Overt versus Institutionalized Discrimination   1
    Legal and Administrative Remedies   2
        The Civil Rights Act and the EEOC   3
        Government Contract Provisions and the OFCC   5
        The Apprenticeship Problem   8
        Quotas and Preferential Treatment   9
        Segregated Seniority Rosters   13
        Conclusions   15
    A Framework for Analysis   18
        Conception of Discrimination   18
        Motives of the Economic Agents   18
        The Actors   20
        Environmental Factors   22
    Notes   24

2   COMBATING EMPLOYMENT DISCRIMINATION IN UNION
    ENTRY AND JOB REFERRAL THROUGH LITIGATION:
    THE CASE OF CONSTRUCTION   26

    Introduction   26
        Plans   27
        Outreach   27
        Law   28

Chapter   Page

    U.S. v. Sheet Metal Workers Local 36 (St. Louis)   28
    Local 53 v. Vogler (New Orleans)   34
    Dobbins v. Local 212 (Cincinnati)   38
    U.S. v. Ironworkers Local 86 (Seattle)   43
    U.S. v. Lathers Local 46 (New York)   51
      Outreach Programs   55
      Contract Compliance Efforts   56
      Other Title VII Litigation   56
    Conclusions   57
    Notes   60

3   COMBATING EMPLOYMENT DISCRIMINATION IN HIRING,
    UPGRADING, AND SENIORITY THROUGH CONTRACT
    COMPLIANCE: THE CASE OF SHIPBUILDING   62

    The Office of Civil Rights in the Maritime Administration   64
    The Newport News Story   66
      The Actors and the Environment: A Southern Setting   68
      The Blumrosen Agreement   69
      The June 12, 1970, Agreement   73
      Overall Changes in Racial Employment Patterns   76
      Summary   80
    Ingalls Shipbuilding Division, Litton Industries   81
      The Course of Events   83
      Growth and Change in Southern Mississippi   88
      Remaining Issues   90
      The Contribution of Outreach   93
      Summary   94
    Alabama Dry Dock and Shipbuilding Company   97
      The Actors and the Environment   97
      The Mobile Economy   98
      The Course of Events   99
      The Affected-Class Settlement   101
      The Overall Magnitude of Recent Change   102
      Summary and Conclusions   107
    Todd Shipyards Corp. and Lockheed Shipbuilding and
      Construction in Seattle   109
      The Actors and the Environment   110
      Continuing Surveillance at the Todd Yard   114
      Continuing Surveillance at the Lockheed Yard   117
      Remaining Issues at Todd and Lockheed   121
      Summary   122
    Postscript   123

Chapter   Page

        Conclusions   134
            The Efficacy of the Office of Civil Rights   134
            The Impact of Local Labor-Market Conditions   136
            The Changing Role of Corporate Personnel Offices   137
            The Role of Organized Labor   137
            The Contribution of Outreach   140
            Women in Shipbuilding   140
            Benchmarks and Training   141
            Affected-Class Settlements: Problems and Prospects   142
        Notes   143

4   SUMMARY AND CONCLUSIONS   144

        Conclusions on Legal Remedies   147
        Conclusions on Contract Compliance   148
        Conceptual Framework: A Final Statement   149

ABOUT THE AUTHORS AND THE CENTER FOR THE STUDY OF
HUMAN RESOURCES   152

LIST OF TABLES AND FIGURES

Table		Page
1.1	Minority Membership in Building Trades, 1972	11
2.1	Imposed Minimum Minority Representation, 1971-75	32
2.2	Minority Representation in the St. Louis Construction Trades, 1972	33
2.3	Value of Building Permits Issued in the City of St. Louis, 1960-72	34
2.4	Minority Representation and Goals for Nonexempt Locals, New Orleans	37
2.5	Minority Representation in the Building Trades Covered by the Cincinnati Plan, October 1974	42
2.6	Construction Activity in the City of Cincinnati, 1966-73	43
2.7	Black Journeymen in Five Seattle Unions, February 1970	44
2.8	Population and Employment in the Seattle SMSA, 1970-73	48
2.9	Apprentices, Graduates, and Goals by Craft, Seattle, December 1975	49
2.10	Employment and Pay Statistics for Local 46, New York, March-July 1970	53
2.11	Construction Volume in Jurisdiction of Local 46, New York, 1967-73	54
2.12	Minority Representation in New York City Construction Trades	56
2.13	Time and Resource Costs of Litigation	58
3.1	U.S. Shipbuilding: Value of Contract Awards Including Major Ship Conversions, by Category of Funding, 1964-74	63
3.2	Rate of Unemployment by Year, Newport News-Hampton Area, 1965-69	69
3.3	Rate of Unemployment by Year, Newport News-Hampton Metropolitan Area, 1970-73	70
3.4	Special Transfer Program Status of Enrollees, Newport News, as of January 1, 1974	75
3.5	Summary of EEO-1 Reports by Date Submitted, Newport News	77
3.6	Unemployment of the Civilian Labor Force, Jackson County, Mississippi, 1961-71	83
3.7	Status of the Affected Class at Ingalls, December 15, 1972	87
3.8	Black Craftsmen at Ingalls, 1969-73	89
3.9	Black Operatives at Ingalls, 1969-73	89

Table		Page
3.10	Black Clericals at Ingalls, 1969–73	90
3.11	East and West Yards Combined, Ingalls, 1973	91
3.12	Female Blue-Collar and Total Blue-Collar Employees at Ingalls, 1973	92
3.13	Placements by RTP at Ingalls, 1971–March 31, 1976	94
3.14	Mobile SMSA Civilian Labor Force and Annual Rates of Unemployment, 1970–73	98
3.15	Current Status of Members of the Affected Class at Alabama Dry Dock Who Moved, September 1974	101
3.16	Disposition of Members of the Affected Class at Alabama Dry Dock Who Did Not Move, September 1974	102
3.17	Modified EEO-1 Form, Alabama Dry Dock, 1964	103
3.18	Modified EEO-1 Form, Alabama Dry Dock, 1970	104
3.19	Modified EEO-1 Form, Alabama Dry Dock, 1973	104
3.20	Modified EEO-1 Form, Alabama Dry Dock, 1974	105
3.21	Employment of Mechanics by Race, Alabama Dry Dock, 1970 and 1973	105
3.22	Promotions among Mechanics by Race, Alabama Dry Dock, 1972	106
3.23	Population and Employment in the Seattle SMSA, 1970–73	110
3.24	Total Employment at Todd-Seattle, October 1969– May 1974	111
3.25	Employment Levels at Lockheed-Seattle, Selected Years, 1966–74	111
3.26	Composition of the Work Force by Sex, Race/Ethnic Group, and Occupational Category at the Todd–Seattle Shipyard, April 1971	112
3.27	Composition of the Work Force by Sex, Race/Ethnic Group, and Occupational Category at the Todd–Seattle Shipyard, May 1974	113
3.28	Todd–Seattle 1971–74 Comparisons: Females to Total	115
3.29	Todd–Seattle 1971–74 Comparisons: Minorities to Total	115
3.30	Minority Participation Rates, Lockheed-Seattle, March 1970– March 1974	117
3.31	Represented Craft Employees, Minorities and Total, Lockheed–Seattle, March 1970–March 1974	117
3.32	Hourly Nonrepresented Employees, Lockheed-Seattle, March 1970–March 1974	118
3.33	Salaried Nonrepresented Employees, Lockheed-Seattle, March 1970–March 1974	118
3.34	Minority Participation in Selected Crafts, Lockheed-Seattle, 1972–74	120

Table		Page
3.35	Female Employees: Total and Minority, Lockheed–Seattle, March 1970–March 1974	121
3.36	Employees by Race, Sex, and Major Job Category, 1974 and 1977, Lockheed Shipbuilding and Construction, Seattle	124
3.37	Employees by Race, Sex, and Major Job Category, 1974 and 1977, Newport News Shipbuilding and Dry Dock Co.	126
3.38	Employees by Race, Sex, and Major Job Category, 1974 and 1977, Ingalls Shipbuilding, Division, Litton Industries	128
3.39	Employees by Race, Sex, and Major Job Category, 1974 and 1977, Alabama Dry Dock and Shipbuilding Co.	130
3.40	Employees by Race, Sex, and Major Job Category, 1974 and 1977, Todd Shipyards Corp., Seattle	132

Figure		
1	Organizational Structure of Office of Civil Rights, Maritime Administration	65

LIST OF ACRONYMS

AFL-CIO	American Federation of Labor and Congress of Industrial Organizations
CCA	Central Contractors Association (Seattle)
CIU	Congress of Independent Unions (St. Louis)
COAC	Court Order Advisory Committee (established in the Ironworkers Local 86 case in Seattle)
EEO	equal employment opportunity
EEOC	Equal Employment Opportunity Commission
FEP	fair employment practices
HRDI	Human Resources Development Institute
IBEW	International Brotherhood of Electrical Workers
JAC	Joint Apprenticeship Committee
JATC	Joint Apprenticeship Training Committee
JET	Journeyman Employment Training program (Cincinnati)
JUMP	Journeyman Union Manpower Program (Cincinnati)
NAACP	National Association for the Advancement of Colored People
NLRB	National Labor Relations Board
OCR	Office of Civil Rights, Maritime Administration
OFCCP	Office of Federal Contract Compliance Programs (formerly Office of Federal Contract Compliance or OFCC)
PREP	Preparation Recruitment Employment Program (Cincinnati)
PREP/JET	The Cincinnati hometown plan which merged PREP and JET
RTP	Recruitment and Training Program
SMSA	Standard Metropolitan Statistical Area
SMW	Sheet Metal Workers International Association
SOIC	Seattle Opportunities Industrialization Council
UCWA	United Construction Workers Association (Seattle)

GLOSSARY OF TERMS

Affected class: a group of people with a common characteristic (race, sex, religion, national origin) who have been denied equal opportunity in violation of Title VII of the Civil Rights Act of 1964. This denial may occur at any step in the employment process: recruitment, placement, promotion, compensation, shift assignment, or working conditions.

Affirmative action plan: a document required of covered government contractors under the regulations of the Office of Federal Contract Compliance Programs. The employer is obliged to compare the participation of minorities and females in the work force with their proportions in the labor market from which workers are drawn to determine if the company is at parity with the labor market. The affirmative action plan is a statement of goals, timetables, and programs indicating how the employer plans to move from its current status to parity.

Carry-forward seniority: provision enabling a worker who transfers from one seniority unit to another to come in with full credit for seniority earned in the previous unit.

Compliance agencies: organizations established under the Office of Federal Contract Compliance Programs, the Department of Labor, or internal subunits of government agencies to which the OFCC has delegated responsibilities. They are charged with the administration of Executive Order 11246 as amended and Revised Orders 4 and 14 and with the analysis and approval of affirmative action plans. Their powers of enforcement include the ability to deny government contracts to employers found in violation.

Conciliation agreement: an agreement reached with the assistance of a third party, who is generally a staff member of the Equal Employment Opportunity Commission or some other agency established to promote equal opportunity. In the conciliation process, the third party acts as intermediary in bringing the parties together without actually deciding or determining the settlement.

Consent decree: a procedure used by the courts to settle a disputed case by having the company or union enter an agreement or understanding on the basis of which litigation will be dismissed in return for taking some sort of action. Once the litigants consent to the entry

---

These definitions are offered for the lay reader and are not to be considered legally definitive.

of a decree and the court has reviewed it, no further appeal is open to the parties.

Line of progression: a grouping of jobs which are related through ladders of promotion. Within a line of progression, workers are upgraded from one job to another on the basis of seniority or some combination of seniority and ability.

Red-circling: a provision whereby a person who transfers from one seniority unit to another retains his or her former rate of pay regardless of relative seniority status or the pay level for the job held in the new unit. However, the transferred worker receives no pay raises until the pay rate in the new unit catches up to the pay level received under the former job. Red-circling had formerly been used in industrial relations to protect workers from downgrading in job reclassification programs.

EMPLOYMENT DISCRIMINATION

1

INTRODUCTION

The primary objective of this study is to investigate the effectiveness of various remedies for discrimination against minorities in employment. Case studies of selected judicial and compliance activities promoting equal employment opportunity (EEO) are presented and analyzed.

This report first addresses judicial remedies pursuant to federal legislation, including Title VII of the 1964 Civil Rights Act. Important cases and out-of-court settlements from various industries covering key employment discrimination issues are analyzed. Chapter 2 focuses on the construction industry, where the predominant issues have been hiring and union entry and job referral procedures.

Chapter 3 examines the efforts of one compliance agency, the Office of Civil Rights, Maritime Administration, in its efforts with five shipbuilding firms. In shipbuilding and ship repair, the chief issues have been entry to craft and supervisory jobs as well as upgrading and seniority systems. Chapter 4 presents a summary and conclusions.

OVERT VERSUS INSTITUTIONALIZED DISCRIMINATION

Before proceeding further, it is useful to define employment discrimination and to describe the economic and social mechanisms through which it is perpetuated. To understand these mechanisms better, one must distinguish between overt and institutionalized forms of employment discrimination.

Discrimination may be overt in the sense that individuals are consciously accorded different treatments in specific cases because of attributes not associated with productivity. Institutional discrimination occurs when people are accorded different treatment because of attributes that are not associated with

1

productivity and that result from the influence of social patterns of behavior to which people have adapted.

In the overt case, for example, applicants for employment might be denied jobs because of their race, national origin, sex, and so on, whereas in the institutional case, applicants might not apply for jobs because of inadequate knowledge of them, a feeling that they would be discriminated against if they did apply, or because segregated educational or training facilities had rendered them unqualified for the position even if overt discrimination were no longer practiced.

Overt discrimination is clearly more easily identified and dealt with. However, in practice, these forms of discrimination might not always be distinct, because there might be some overlap, as when discriminators use their knowledge of institutionalized behavior patterns to practice overt discrimination.

Discrimination might also take many forms. In this study, we are concerned mainly with employment discrimination against racial or ethnic minorities. Although the policies concerned also are applicable to women and other groups, the same analytical consideration will not necessarily apply to these groups. Before looking at our specific case studies, we will outline the development of legal remedies with respect to discrimination.

LEGAL AND ADMINISTRATIVE REMEDIES

Since World War II, enforceable laws against discrimination have been passed in over half of the states and many municipalities. These laws cover virtually the entire black population outside the South, where only Kentucky had adopted such a statute by 1975. Generally, these laws are administered by part-time commissioners who ordinarily have powers to receive, investigate, and pass on complaints; use conferences, conciliation, and persuasion in an effort to resolve complaints; conduct public hearings, subpoena witnesses, and compel their attendance under oath as well as requiring the production of records relating to matters before the hearings; seek court orders enforcing subpoenas or requesting cease-and-desist orders; and undertake and publish studies of discrimination.

Before the Civil Rights Act of 1964, blacks also used the courts to combat discrimination in employment. Most court cases dealt with unions, because in the absence of statutes or nondiscrimination clauses in collective bargaining or government contracts, employers had no legal obligation not to discriminate.

Unions acquired legal rights and duties as a result of the National Labor Relations and Railway Labor Acts. Specifically, in the 1944 Steele decision

(323 U.S. 192 [1944]), the Supreme Court ruled that the Constitution imposed upon unions that acquired the privilege of exclusive bargaining rights the duty to represent all members of the bargaining unit fairly. Aggrieved minorities have, therefore, brought legal action for injunctions and damages against discriminating unions.

Moreover, in the 1964 Hughes Tool case (147 NLRB 1573 [1964]), the National Labor Relations Board (NLRB) held violation of the duty of fair representation to be an unfair labor practice, giving aggrieved minorities a measure of administrative relief by permitting them to file charges with the NLRB instead of with the courts.

The major antidiscrimination measures applicable to employers before the 1964 Civil Rights Act were the nondiscrimination clauses required in contracts with the federal government. These nondiscrimination provisions were required by executive orders issued by various presidents beginning with Franklin D. Roosevelt during World War II.

The Civil Rights Act and the EEOC

The main statute, however, against discrimination in the United States is the Civil Rights Act of 1964. Title VII of that act outlawed discrimination on the basis of race, color, religion, sex, or national origin in hiring, compensation, and promotion. The law applies to private employers, state and local governments, government organizations, educational institutions, employment agencies, and labor organizations employing or serving 15 or more persons.

The Equal Employment Opportunity Commission (EEOC) was created to enforce Title VII. Under the 1964 act, the commission's role was limited to investigating charges, issuing cause or no-cause findings, attempting conciliation between charging parties and respondents, and, failing that, filing "friend of the court" briefs for those charging parties who exercised their right under the act to seek redress in federal court. Title VII authorized the attorney general to bring suit against respondents under a special section of the act. The EEOC established a reporting system pursuant to the act and provided technical assistance for voluntary compliance to employers and unions.

Amendments in 1972 extended the act's coverage into the public sector and empowered the EEOC to bring civil actions in federal court seeking remedies on behalf of charging parties. The 1972 amendments also shifted litigation functions (some with a two-year delay) from the Department of Justice to the EEOC.

The number of charges of discrimination filed with the EEOC nearly tripled between 1970 and 1973, when it reached over 47,000. Approximately 60 percent alleged racial discrimination. Over 85 percent of the complaints were against employers; the rest were against unions, employment agencies, and other parties.

Complaints of racial discrimination usually involved a refusal to hire, a discharge, or an inferior job classification. Charges of exclusion from unions were relatively rare, accounting for only 4 percent of the racial discrimination charges against unions; complaints about discrimination in referrals were more common.

Despite its case load, the EEOC did not have a major impact on employment practices during its first six years. Before the 1972 amendments, the commission relied primarily on conciliation and voluntary agreements to comply with Title VII; formal decisions were less frequent. The procedures were time-consuming and uncertain; and the results were meager. In fiscal 1972 the commission completed action on over 2,800 cases without a formal decision, and written agreements were achieved in only 412 cases. Of the 970 cases closed after a decision, 314 resulted in agreements.

Conciliation agreements had no legal force and thus often caused limited employment changes. For example, a study comparing firms charged with discrimination by the EEOC with others not charged found that only one in four of those charged had a better minority employment record than its counterpart firms.

In addition, the overall effects of the EEOC were usually not discernible. In Memphis, Tennessee, where 16 successful conciliations were negotiated in 1967 and 1968, minority employment among employers subject to the law increased only from 29.1 percent to 29.7 percent for men between 1966 and 1969. In Atlanta, Georgia, where eight conciliations were successful during 1967 and 1968, minority employment among males dropped from 16.5 percent to 16 percent.[1] Of course, employment patterns are influenced by labor-market considerations, which often were much stronger than the limited effects of the EEOC.

It is important, however, to distinguish the direct and indirect effects of Title VII and other antidiscrimination activities. Perhaps the greatest impact of law is not the direct enforcement activities but the tendency they create among some employers to comply with the law. This effect is probably greatest where employers already have strong economic motives to hire those discriminated against but are deterred from making the changes due to fear of adverse reaction from customers or current employees. In these cases, the law provides an excuse for taking the desired action.

Although basic Title VII compliance procedures remained unchanged between 1964 and March 1972, when the expanded powers became law, court decisions strengthened the EEOC's power. During the early years after the Civil Rights Act was passed, the courts were preoccupied with procedural matters (time limits for filing charges, right of the EEOC to intervene, and class action suits), but they turned to more substantive issues during the late 1960s and early 1970s.

In 1971 the Supreme Court ruled unanimously (*Griggs v. Duke Power Co.*) that Title VII "proscribes not only overt discrimination but also practices that are fair in form, but discriminatory in operation." Preemployment tests that were not proved to be job-related were outlawed as arbitrary and discriminatory where the tests excluded blacks and other minorities. The precedent was expanded to other job requirements that were not business necessities.

The Griggs case was also important because the Supreme Court dealt with the question of the *effects* rather than the invidious *intent* of discriminatory practices. (Supreme Court rulings in 1977 in cases regarding discrimination in housing and education seem to have returned to a focus on intent rather than effects, however.)

The Court also ruled (*Gregory v. Litton Systems, Inc.*) that a company's refusal to employ people with a number of arrests, but not convictions, was discriminatory because blacks are statistically more likely to be arrested than whites. Perhaps most significantly, a landmark case in 1971 (*Robinson v. Lorillard Co.*) established the principle of monetary relief in class-action cases and raised the prospect of substantial settlement costs.[2]

The commission's new potential for filing class actions with large settlements caused considerable concern among employers. Many who feared that conciliation activities might be abandoned in favor of litigation became much more amenable to conciliation.

In 1973 the American Telephone and Telegraph Company (AT&T) signed a consent decree providing $15 million in restitution and back pay for several classes of female employees plus a $23 million promotion package for women and minorities.[3] This agreement was part of a campaign to improve employment opportunities for women and minorities and was based on a novel approach whereby the company's right to a rate increase by the Federal Power Commission was challenged because of noncompliance with Title VII.

In addition, the EEOC's legal staff was increased more than fivefold in the first six months of 1973. In order to have the maximum effect, priority was assigned to cases involving major companies and unions with large numbers of outstanding charges against them.

Government Contract Provisions and the OFCC

Another way to promote equal employment opportunity is to use antidiscrimination clauses in government contracts. The Office of Federal Contract Compliance (OFCC) in the Department of Labor is responsible for administering this program. The OFCC was created in 1965 by Executive Order 11246, which prohibited discrimination by government contractors on the basis of race, creed, color, or national origin. In 1967, sex was added to this list by Executive Order 11375.

In February 1970 the OFCC issued orders requiring contractors to examine their utilization of minority workers, to establish "affirmative action" goals and timetables for hiring designated proportions of minorities, and to collect data to demonstrate their progress. In December 1971 this order was amended to include sex discrimination. These enforcement powers apply to companies employing an estimated one-third of the labor force.

The OFCC's enforcement powers include the ability to cancel, terminate, or suspend current contracts and to debar offenders from future participation in government contracts. But the OFCC has not fully utilized these powers; it has limited its enforcement activities to requiring affirmative action plans by contractors and unions. By April 1975, in only 11 cases had contractors been debarred.[4]

A number of factors have limited the OFCC's ability to change racial employment patterns. The most important of these are associated with collective bargaining procedures and labor-market institutions. The OFCC is particularly limited by its inability to bring action directly against labor organizations (because the latter are not parties to federal contracts).

Moreover, many employment practices have been structured by collective bargaining contracts. Changing racial patterns might, therefore, require alterations in contractual relationships which protect white workers as well as black. White workers are, therefore, likely to resist these changes.

For example, in 1967 at the Sparrows Point, Mayland, plant of the Bethlehem Steel Company, the OFCC found that 80 percent of the black employees were working in 14 of the plant's dirtiest and hottest departments, with limited advancement opportunities. To transfer to a department with better job progression, blacks were required to start at the bottom, frequently losing seniority and taking wage reductions.

Following its findings of discriminatory practices in 1967 at Bethlehem, the Department of Labor initiated a hearing process with a three-member panel. Work began in 1968, but a final report was delayed until December 1970. The panel found that the company was guilty of discriminatory practices but voted two to one to forego any remedy because, on business necessity grounds, it would have been "too disruptive."

Subsequently, the secretary of labor took charge and solicited more information from interested parties; the Department of Labor issued an order on January 15, 1973. There was, however, further delay in that the order was not implemented until October 15, 1973. The order posting the remedy allowed black steelworkers in 14 departments to transfer with rate retention and to carry forward seniority. The remedy allowed two bidding systems, one of which called for plantwide seniority if a member of the affected class was involved in the bidding process. This rule was applied in promotions, layoff, and recall. Unfortunately, shortly before the ruling took effect, the company announced a layoff; the new layoff rules, which applied where members of the affected class were involved, produced bitterness among both white and black workers. The excessive delay and the problems that surfaced in the implementation process provided some useful lessons for practitioners in this field.

The experience of the Bethlehem plants at Lackawanna and at Sparrows Point led Judge Pointer to avoid any use of dual bidding procedures in the remedy provided in the Fairfield case.[5] This kind of remedy was approved by the same court in the consent decree that covered nine steel companies and the international union.

Change also is limited because blacks often do not respond to changes as much as their initiators expect. For example, as a result of a 1971 Department of Justice suit, 1,600 black employees in Bethlehem's Lackawanna plant were granted transfer rights. Given four months to sign up, only 430 did so, and only 70 actually changed jobs. Some were unqualified for the new positions; some senior black workers saw no advantage in moving as they approached retirement; others preferred to stay where they were. Clearly, well-entrenched institutional discrimination cannot be erased easily by judicial decree.

The seniority issue illustrates the problems involved in changing institutionalized patterns in industrial situations, but other problems exist in the construction industry, where seniority is relatively less important. In the building trades, blacks have been underrepresented in those crafts paying the highest wages.

To change this situation, the Department of Labor initiated a number of plans which established goals and timetables designed to bring the black employment share of skilled workers up to their proportion in the metropolitan population. Despite goals and timetables, however, none of these plans was very successful in achieving its objectives.

Major reasons for failure were rising unemployment, as the recession hit construction harder than other sectors, and a lack of effective machinery to translate goals and timetables into more positions in the construction labor market. The plans established goals and timetables for particular federal construction projects, which was not the same as attaching workers to a labor market.

In 1974, in an action which some observers feel—along with the AT&T settlement mentioned earlier—might greatly improve employment opportunities for women and minorities, nine major companies and the United Steelworkers of America entered into a consent decree to end a lawsuit filed by the Department of Justice on behalf of Peter J. Brennan, secretary of labor, and the EEOC. In the settlement, the union and the companies agreed to pay 40,000 minority and women workers $30.9 million in back pay and to establish goals and timetables to increase the number of such workers in areas where they had been underrepresented.

Meeting these goals is estimated to cost the companies millions of dollars in higher wages for women and minority workers, who were given preference in moving into previously "white male" jobs until the goals were reached. A tripartite (union/industry/government) "audit and review" committee was established to monitor compliance with the program for five years. At each plant, company/union/minority "implementation committees" were established to ensure compliance with goals and timetables.

The union and the companies entered into the consent decree in order to avoid what they considered to be the danger that the industrywide lawsuit would lead to widespread disruption of seniority rules, the substitution of unworkable regulations written by judges, the threatened bankruptcy of many local unions, and a possible severe crippling of the international union. The negotiated settlement minimized these dangers. (The only major company refusing to accept the consent decree was Inland Steel, which objected to the implication that it had practiced discrimination in employment.)

The Apprenticeship Problem

Civil rights leaders have concentrated on apprenticeship because this system leads to good jobs in the skilled trades and because there have been very few blacks in them, in part because institutional discrimination influenced many black youngsters not to attempt to enter apprenticeship programs before the 1960s.

The craft unions' recruitment patterns excluded most black youths from any opportunity to enter the system. Blacks also were disadvantaged in meeting the qualifications for entry into apprenticeship programs. Many programs require a high school education, and not only does the education level of nonwhites still lag behind that of whites, but many blacks have been handicapped by what Kenneth Clark calls "the massive inefficiency of the public schools where the masses of Negroes go."[6]

In 1963, Secretary of Labor Willard Wirtz approved new federal apprenticeship standards designed to provide "full and fair opportunity for application." These regulations had limited impact for a variety of reasons but basically because few blacks applied for or could meet the qualifications and testing procedures.

The Bureau of Apprenticeship and Training (BAT), which administers the program, also has limited enforcement powers. Deregistration, BAT's main weapon, is more of an inconvenience than a serious deterrent to discrimination.[7]

Legal sanctions were not especially successful, although they have perhaps had the effect of creating among apprenticeship sponsors a climate conducive to change; apprenticeship standards and programs have become more formalized; some apprenticeship sponsors have raised their qualifications.

The possibility of sanctions also seems to have strengthened "voluntary" compliance programs. Although sanctions have been used very rarely (because relatively few formal written complaints have been lodged against discrimination in apprenticeship training and because discrimination is difficult to prove), anti-discrimination agencies have succeeded in making investigations that have clarified the extent of black participation in apprenticeship programs and have focused attention on some of the problems involved in increasing the number of black apprentices.

The limitations of legal sanctions led to the creation of apprenticeship information centers (to distribute information about apprenticeship programs) and outreach programs to recruit, tutor, and place apprentices. These programs have been fairly successful in increasing the number and proportion of minority apprentices. These programs have been operated primarily by the RTP (Recruitment and Training Program, formerly the Workers Defense League), the National Urban League, building trades councils of the AFL-CIO* Human Resources Development Institute, and other local organizations in some places.

Largely as a result of these outreach programs, the proportion of all apprentices who are members of minority groups has increased steadily since 1960, when minorities accounted for only 2.5 percent of all apprentices.[8] They accounted for 4.4 percent in 1966, 8 percent in 1969, and over 14 percent in 1973. Minorities accounted for only 6 percent of all new apprentices in 1967 but 17 percent of new apprentices in 1973 and 1974. In July 1974, when Secretary of Labor Peter Brennan reactivated the Federal Committee on Apprenticeship (which had not met for five years), he announced that outreach programs had recruited and registered 30,000 apprentices since 1968.

Although apprenticeship outreach programs have been more successful than any other approach to this problem, it remains to be seen if they can cause the kinds of changes throughout the country that will replace institutionalized discrimination with institutionalized equal opportunity. So far, however, they have demonstrated the importance of a comprehensive approach to recruiting and preparing black youngsters for apprenticeship programs. Moreover, this approach has demonstrated its effectiveness in getting blacks into other jobs more easily and at lower costs.

Quotas and Preferential Treatment

Various programs to increase black employment opportunities in the construction and other industries have raised the highly controversial legal and moral issue of quotas and preferential treatment. Policies proposed by some civil rights leaders and government agencies are based on the belief that progress in

---

*American Federation of Labor and Congress of Industrial Organizations.

eliminating patterns of inequality requires compensation for past discrimination. However, unions and employers have resisted these efforts on the grounds that they discriminate against white workers and cause inefficiency.

Court challenge of the Philadelphia plan, which required goals and time-tables in the construction industry, was initiated by the Contractors Association of Eastern Pennsylvania, which charged that the plan violated the Constitution and the laws of both the United States and Pennsylvania. However, in 1970 a federal district court in Pennsylvania upheld the plan as valid under Title VII and the Constitution.

The court pointed out that the concept of "affirmative action" had been upheld as a valid exercise of presidential powers in a number of cases and added:

> The heartbeat of "affirmative action" is the policy of developing programs which shall provide in detail for specific steps to guarantee equal employment opportunity. The Philadelphia Plan is no more or less than a means for implementation of the affirmative action obligations of Executive Order 11246.

Moreover, according to the court:

> The plan does not require the contractor to hire a definite percentage of a minority group. To the contrary, it merely requires that he make every good faith effort to meet his commitment to attain certain goals. If a contractor is unable to meet the goal, but has exhibited good faith, then the imposition of sanctions, in our opinion, would be subject to judicial review (*Contractors Association of Eastern Pennsylvania v. Shultz*, D.C.E., 1970).

Thus the court argued, in effect, that the establishment of goals is legal but that an attempt to force an employer to meet those goals might be illegal. Because such argument turns on the definition of "good faith" and the procedures to determine qualifications and standards, the issues involved in the Philadelphia plan obviously have not been settled. In October 1971 the Supreme Court refused to review this case, letting the lower court ruling stand. While pushing variations of the Philadelphia plan, the Department of Labor has also accepted voluntary or "hometown" plans.

However, in July 1974, after dissatisfaction with the results of so-called hometown plans for voluntary efforts to change racial employment patterns in the construction industry, the Department of Labor imposed mandatory hiring goals on 101 building trades unions involved in 21 hometown plans. These goals were imposed after the OFCC determined that the participants in these places were not making a good-faith effort to meet voluntary standards for increasing minority participation. The OFCC did not release statistics showing the extent to which the hometown plans had failed, but a 1973 survey of 31 of 70 government-approved plans showed that less than one-third of the local unions had met their goals.

At about the time the OFCC imposed the mandatory goals, the EEOC released figures showing that minority membership in building trades unions reporting to that agency increased by 2.4 percent between 1969 and 1972. Minority membership was much greater relatively in the laborers, painters, roofers, and trowel and miscellaneous trades than it was in the more highly skilled mechanical crafts, as indicated by Table 1.1, showing EEOC statistics for 1972. These patterns are not unlike those of other industries where minorities are heavily concentrated among the lower-paying occupations. If anything, few other industries afford minorities relatively as many high-paying opportunities as the building trades.

TABLE 1.1

Minority Membership in Building Trades, 1972

Trade Classification	Total Union Membership	Minority* Percent
Mechanical trades	600,049	6.9
Boilermakers	32,804	11.4
Electrical workers	2?7,719	7.5
Elevator constructors	9,066	5.5
Iron workers	84,931	9.3
Plumbers, pipefitters	189,814	4.2
Sheetmetal workers	45,715	6.9
Trowel and miscellaneous trades	626,609	10.7
Asbestos workers	9,569	3.7
Bricklayers	32,646	13.1
Carpenters	366,215	11.4
Lathers	2,978	14.2
Marble polishers	3,125	15.2
Operating engineers	183,207	6.2
Plasterers and masons	28,869	32.5
Laborers, painters, and roofers	377,793	37.5
Laborers	295,563	43.4
Painters	67,446	14.8
Roofers	14,784	23.4
Total building trades	1,604,451	15.6

*Minority refers to blacks, Spanish-surnamed Americans, Asian Americans, and American Indians.

Source: U.S. Equal Employment Opportunity Commission news release, dated June 30, 1974.

The debate over the Philadelphia plan did not resolve the issues, in part because the protagonists addressed themselves to different questions. The defenders of the programs argued for the legality of the executive order and affirmative action, not whether "quotas" or "goals" could legally be imposed; opponents of the plan argued that it required quotas—which was not the case, at least in the sense that employers would lose contracts for failing to hire a fixed number of black craft workers.

Although the "qualifications" question is a key factor in minority participation in building trades, it was given inadequate attention during conflict with the construction industry over black employment. This question is important, because in the absence of some agreement over the definition of qualifications for a particular craft, it is difficult to see how black workers in those crafts are to be identified and put to work.

Although the technical difficulties involved probably account for the inadequate attention to this question, other factors undoubtedly are at work as well. For one thing, a prevailing assumption seems to be that there are many fully qualified black construction workers who are ready to be put to work who are unemployed or underemplyed because of discrimination. To some extent, this idea rests on the belief that the construction industry has exaggerated its qualifications for discriminatory reasons. There also seems to be a middle-class bias that qualifications and standards really are not too important for manual crafts—an assumption that *all* manual jobs are of low status and therefore do not really require mathematics or a four-year apprenticeship.

Of course, what many people fear is that quotas and preferential treatment will cause blacks with less than the minimum required qualifications to be hired ahead of more qualified whites in order to compensate blacks for past discrimination. Regardless of its short-run consequences, this kind of "preferential treatment" has serious long-run implications. No better statement of this point can be made than the following comment by the noted psychologist Kenneth Clark:

> I cannot express vehemently enough my abhorrence of sentimentalistic, seemingly compassionate programs of employment of Negroes which employ them on Jim Crow double standards or special standards for the Negro which are lower than those for whites.
>
> This is a perpetuation of racism—it is interpreted by the Negro as condescension, and it will be exploited by them. Those who have been neglected and deprived must understand that they are being taken seriously as human beings. They must not be regarded as peculiar human beings who cannot meet the demands more privileged human beings meet. . . . I suspect that the significant breakdown in the efficiency of American public education came not primarily from flagrant racial bigotry and the deliberate desire to

create casualties but from the good intentions, namely, the sloppy sentimentalistic good intentions of educators to reduce standards of low-income and minority group youngsters.[9]

Segregated Seniority Rosters

Efforts to desegregate or integrate seniority rosters have involved many issues similar to those raised in the construction industry as well as some that are unique. Indeed, in many ways the seniority question is more complex than the issues raised by minority participation in the construction industry. This is an important area because of the prevalence of job segregation, especially in the South, where institutionalized discrimination confined blacks to agriculture and the most menial or undesirable nonagricultural jobs, and because desegregation is essential to significant improvements in black employment patterns.

The main issues raised by the seniority question relate to whether blacks are to be compensated for past discrimination when seniority rosters are merged; whether company or plant seniority will be used for blacks alone or for blacks and whites; whether such impediments as wage reductions, time limitations, and loss of pay will be permitted to deter integration; and whether blacks will be required to pass special tests which whites already in the line did not have to pass.

Considerable attention was devoted to the segregated seniority issue by various government contracting committees during and after World War II. However, the impact of the contracting committees was limited by their inherent weaknesses and the fact that they concentrated on industries, like petroleum refining, where blue-collar employment was declining.

By the time of the Civil Rights Act, only token integration of blacks had taken place in major southern manufacturing plants. In addition to the factors mentioned above, seniority integration was impeded by the fact that many blacks hired as laborers lacked the education and experience to move up. Conversely, many senior blacks would have been forced to accept lower wages and lose job seniority in order to enter the bottom jobs in previously all-white lines of progression. Because seniority is a jealously guarded right and influences the profitability of industrial plants, it is not surprising that the terms under which seniority rosters are desegregated should be such a controversial and complex issue.

An important pre-Civil Rights Act decision came in the 1959 Whitfield case, where the Fifth Circuit Court of Appeals ruled that it was legal for unions to permit blacks to transfer to the bottom of formerly all-white lines of progression (*Whitfield v. United Steelworkers*). However, the Whitfield decision has not been followed in a series of post-Civil Rights Act cases.

In the 1968 Quarles case, departmental seniority at the Phillip Morris plant in Richmond was held not to have been illegal per se. However, a system based on previous discriminatory practices was not legal if "employers maintain differences in employee operations which were the result of discrimination before the Act went into effect" (*Quarles v. Phillip Morris*). In this case, "the restrictive departmental transfer and seniority provisions . . . are intentional, unlawful employment practices because they are imposed on a departmental structure that was organized on a racially segregated basis."

The court also concluded that Title VII of the Civil Rights Act "does not require that Negroes be preferred over white employees who possess employment seniority. It is also apparent that the Congress did not intend to freeze an entire generation of Negro employees into discriminatory patterns that existed before the Act." The court required the company to permit permanent black employees who had been discriminated against to transfer into formerly all-white departments on the basis of company seniority. However, the Quarles decision, which has been relied on in other cases (*Irvin v. Mohawk Rubber Co.*, 1970), reduced the seniority rights of temporary black employees and did not disturb the departmental seniority system.[10]

Partly because the Supreme Court refused to review it, the Crown Zellerbach case has been regarded as a landmark decision by many civil rights leaders (*U.S. v. United Paper Makers*, 1969; *Hicks v. Crown Zellerbach Corp.*, 1968). In this case, brought by the Department of Justice under Title VII and Executive Order 11246, a federal district court ruled that a departmental seniority arrangement at the company's plant in Bogalusa, Louisiana, violated the Civil Rights Act.

As in Quarles, the court held that blacks who had been discriminated against could be promoted to jobs they were qualified to perform on the basis of company and not departmental seniority. Moreover, the court held that "institutional systems or procedures which deny to Negroes advancement to jobs held by whites with comparable mill seniority and ability consistent with [the] employer's interest in maintaining [the] skill and efficiency of [its] labor force . . . must be removed."

These institutional arrangements included prohibitions on promotions of more than one job slot at a time where intermediate jobs did not afford training necessary for the next higher jobs or where employees had acquired the necessary training through temporary assignments; requiring black employees to enter the previously all-white lines of progression at below those steps necessary to provide training for the next higher jobs; limiting time intervals for promotion to periods longer than necessary to learn the job before promotion; and "deterring Negro employees from transferring to formerly all-white lines of progression by requiring these employees to suffer a reduction in wages and a loss of promotional security as a condition of transfer."[11]

Federal courts have ruled a number of times on the applicability of collective bargaining provisions to civil rights remedies. In *Alexander v. Gardner-Denver Co.* (415 U.S. 36 [1974]), the Supreme Court ruled that employees did not foreclose their Title VII rights to trial de novo by prior submission of issues to final arbitration:

> the federal policy favoring arbitration of labor disputes and the federal policy against discriminatory employment practices can best be accommodated by permitting an employee to pursue fully both his remedy under the grievance-arbitration clause of a collective bargaining agreement and his cause of action under Title VII. The federal court should consider the employee's claim de novo.

One of the most important recent issues involved in the conflict between collective bargaining agreements and affirmative action plans was demonstrated in *Jersey Central Power and Light v. IBEW Local Union* (No. 74-2016, F.2d, 1975), and *Watkins v. United Steelworkers Local 2369* (No. 72-2604, F.2d, July 16, 1975)—cases in which the circuit courts òf appeals reversed lower court rulings that conciliation agreements should be enforced in such a way that layoffs would result in the retention of minority workers in the proportion they were represented in the prelayoff peak.

The appeals court ruled that the collective bargaining agreement gave senior workers priority in layoffs over junior women and minorities. In the Watkins case, the court ruled that seniority agreements resulting in the discharge of more blacks than whites did not violate Title VII. If upheld by the Supreme Court, these rulings will limit the ability of both the OFCC and the EEOC to require the retention of women and minorities during layoffs.

Conclusions

Although the courts' rulings on the question of the remedies for discrimination in seniority systems might appear confusing and although many of the issues remain to be resolved by the Supreme Court, some consistent threads seem to be emerging. With respect to imposition of affirmative action programs to correct pre-Civil Rights Act discrimination, the courts seem clearly to have held that no penalties can be imposed for preact discrimination but that procedures adopted before the act cannot be continued where the procedure was clearly adopted for discriminatory purposes and perpetuates discrimination, as was the case in Quarles and Crown Zellerbach. However, in both of these cases and in Griggs (*U.S. v. Duke Power Company*, 1971), the courts recognized that there might be legitimate business reasons for retaining the seniority system (that is, job security).

The forms of employment discrimination most resistant to legal pressures are of the institutionalized variety. The key issues addressed in this study are predominantly institutional. Previous studies as well as the cases presented in this study demonstrate that overt issues (for example, the use of separate dressing facilities) yield more readily to the force of law.

The main reasons for this are fairly obvious in a legal system based on due process. The state ordinarily prosecutes those who break laws, and in a system characterized by due process, the burden of proof is on the state. Therefore, if there is a law or contractual obligation not to discriminate, people who violate the laws or their contractual obligations must pay the penalty prescribed by law, but the government must prove that the accused has in fact violated the law. Overt acts are more obvious and therefore more conducive to proof.

Institutionalized patterns of behavior, on the other hand, are not necessarily in violation of the law and are therefore less likely to yield to the case-by-case approach characteristic of the U.S. legal system. Since institutional forms of discrimination have been so pervasive, the legal system would be even more overloaded than it is if all cases of institutional discrimination were prosecuted. Moreover, as this study will demonstrate, serious constitutional and legal issues are raised by attempts to use our legal system—designed primarily to prevent overt acts—to change institutionalized patterns of behavior with respect to discrimination.

Let us briefly review research conducted thus far regarding the efficacy of legal antidiscrimination activities, including contract compliance among government contractors.

Considerable attention has been devoted to measuring the effect of public antidiscrimination activities on minority employment, but less has been given to assessing the impact of these activities on the employment of women. Much of the early work focused on the efficacy of state and local antidiscrimination legislation. The findings indicated that notwithstanding the dedication of many staff and commission members, the performance of most state and local fair employment practices commissions (FEPC) has not been impressive.

From a survey of this research in 1970, Dale Hiestand concluded that the efforts generally have not been very successful.[12] With few exceptions,[13] research indicates that relative to whites, minority employment gains in states and cities with FEP (fair employment practices) laws have generally been small.[14]

The weakness of many state and local FEP laws and their enforcement is frequently cited as a reason for this finding. Several studies conclude that where FEP legislation has been enforced vigorously and consistently, its effect has been beneficial.[15] However, these results should be interpreted with caution, since active enforcement of FEP legislation may coincide with a more favorable climate toward minorities. Thus the observed improvement in minority employment positions may be attributable to other factors rather than the enforcement of FEP legislation.

The performance of federal antidiscrimination efforts also has been less than impressive. As noted earlier, prior to amendment of the law providing the

EEOC with enforcement powers, the EEOC was generally unsuccessful in securing voluntary compliance with Title VII through conciliation and persuasion.[16]

Only one out of three respondents charged with employment discrimination prior to 1972—where reasonable cause existed to believe the charge to be true—agreed voluntarily to change its alleged discriminatory employment practices.[17] Among respondents agreeing to this change, minority employment gains were generally small.[18] Similar findings are reported in studies of the textile[19] and construction[20] industries.

Antidiscrimination legislation may affect the employment practices not only of firms charged with unlawful employment discrimination but of organizations not charged who wish to avoid prosecution or who are otherwise motivated to comply with the law. Consequently, several studies have examined the combined influence of these effects of changes in the labor market for minority groups, specifically black Americans.[21]

Richard B. Freeman concludes that much of the improvement in the black economic position that took place in the late 1960s appears to be the result of governmental and related antidiscriminatory activity associated with Title VII.[22] Again, however, as in the earlier case of state and local FEP legislation, Freeman is unable to separate the influence of the law from that of the coincident period of sustained economic activity and intense civil rights demonstrations.

Indeed, a careful examination of the evidence casts considerable doubt on Freeman's conclusion.[23] The changes in black employment during the last half of the 1960s can more logically be attributed to economic and labor-market conditions than to enforcement activities of the EEOC. In the first place, the EEOC did not have strong enforcement powers during this period. Moreover, the commission had very limited resources and a serious case backlog.

A better hypothesis would therefore be that many employers and unions had strong economic motives for hiring blacks and women and used the law as an excuse for doing so. An excuse was needed because before it became illegal to discriminate, employers apparently were sufficiently concerned about adverse reactions from white customers or employees that they would not hire blacks even when it might otherwise have been profitable for them to do so. A major objective of our study is to examine the precise conditions under which those responsible for racial employment patterns will change behavior and the role that law plays in causing these changes.

Likewise, federal EEO compliance activities pursuant to Executive Order 11246 have been subject to evaluation by the General Accounting Office,[24] the U.S. Commission on Civil Rights,[25] and various econometricians. The econometric studies evaluate impact by comparing the EEO performance of government contractors with noncontractors in the aggregate. Such studies conclude that the overall compliance activity through 1972 had been minimal at best.[26] The Commission on Civil Rights and the General Accounting Office studies indicate that such results may be due to insufficient implementation of the executive order. Both point to inadequacies and failures in the compliance process as it operates in practice.

A FRAMEWORK FOR ANALYSIS

In our previous work on black employment patterns and remedies to improve black employment patterns,[27] we have found a systems framework which is much better than the orthodox or neoclassical economic theory of discrimination for viewing labor-market discrimination. A systems framework is more relevant and useful, because it provides an understanding for the basic forces causing and perpetuating institutional discrimination as well as insight for developing appropriate antidiscrimination policies.

Conception of Discrimination

In order to make it fit the wage-theory mold, orthodox economists define discrimination as a taste for which an economic agent acts, as if he were willing to pay something "to be associated with some persons rather than others." This definition creates a number of conceptual problems.

First, it assumes discrimination to be a "physical" phenomenon—a desire by whites, for example, not to associate with blacks, which scarcely conforms with reality, where whites have been in close physical association with blacks. Clearly, discrimination is more a status or caste phenomenon, a concept which makes the theory more general, because the physical phenomenon surely cannot be applied to sexual discrimination. Discriminators object to discriminatees partly because the latter are generally regarded to be "inferior" people who would lower the status of the discriminators.

Motives of the Economic Agents

But a theory of discrimination should show how discrimination interacts with the motives of certain actors. The neoclassical model does this, in part, by assuming that actors with "discrimination coefficients" modify the usual motives specified in the neoclassical utility functions. The model assumes, we think correctly, that employers are motivated mainly by profits but that this motive is modified by a "taste for discrimination" or a "perception of reality."

If the model assumes "physical association" to be a problem, it is difficult to see why employers, especially in large firms, would discriminate against blue-collar workers, with whom employers would not be associating. However, it is possible that discrimination by employees could be transmitted to employers, causing them to act *as if* they had discrimination coefficients themselves. If employers have status motives for discrimination, they would not object to hiring discriminatees for "inferior" jobs but would object to hiring them for higher-status jobs.

The neoclassical model also seems to make unrealistic assumptions about the motives of white workers, who probably are more responsible than employers for discrimination in blue-collar jobs. The neoclassicists assume that white workers with discriminatory attitudes are mainly motivated by wage rates. This assumption leads to some curious results.

First, white workers are presumed to demand higher wages to work with blacks who are perfect substitutes. That is curious in view of the usual neoclassical assumption that people act rationally, because surely white workers could see that such demands would be self-defeating, because blacks would displace whites. White workers are more likely to demand that blacks be excluded entirely from "status" jobs than to demand racial wage differentials.

Moreover, the white workers' basic motivation is likely to be job control rather than wage rates. The wage rate is an important part of the job, but the job's status, working conditions, stability, opportunity for advancement, and the extent to which workers participate in the formulation of job rules are also important considerations. Discriminators are likely to want to monopolize the better jobs for themselves and will use race, sex, and so on, as a means for doing so.

The conceptual framework we have found useful for policy analyses of discrimination specifies the motives of the various actors and the contexts within which they operate on the basis of empirical evidence rather than a priori deductive reasoning. Our formulation could be called a "systems" model and is similar to that developed for industrial relations by John Dunlop in his *Industrial Relations Systems.*[28]

However, it is not possible to present a definitive comparison of this alternative formulation with the neoclassical model, because they have different objectives. Our approach is less designed to be compatible with a general equilibrium model and therefore is less rigorous but, hopefully, more relevant for understanding the basic forces causing and perpetuating discrimination and affords more insight into appropriate antidiscrimination policies. Each group of actors in the racial employment process develops mechanisms to improve its power relative to the others. In this formulation, wages merely constitute one aspect of the job.

Second, a systems model assumes racial employment patterns in any given situation to be products of the power relationship between the actors and the specific environmental contexts within which they operate. These relationships between the actors and the specific environmental contexts can be empirically determined to some extent and, while relatively stable in the short run, change through time and involve dynamic mutual causation rather than one-way causal relationships.

The Actors

The main actors involved in the determination of racial employment patterns are managers, white workers, black workers, unions, and government agencies responsible for the implementation of antidiscrimination and industrial relations policies.

The main environmental features influencing racial employment patterns include economic and labor market conditions, community race relations, the distribution of power in the larger community, industry structure and growth potential, the labor market skills, education of black and white populations and the requirements of various companies and industries, and the operation of labor market institutions.

Employers

We have argued that an employer's main motive is profit maximization and status. However, profit maximization must be considered in a much broader context than the effect of individual marginal productivities on wages.

Management hiring decisions also will be influenced by firm size, industry structure, and the nature of labor supplies. The strongest factor influencing the black workers' ability to combat discrimination is not marginal productivity of each worker but total labor supplies to meet management's requirements if whites strike or boycott. In the systems model, larger supplies of labor increase bargaining power. Whites rarely will be able to exclude large supplies of blacks qualified to take their place.

Moreover, where there are adequate total labor supplies, employers frequently prefer minority workers for certain kinds of jobs, because the limited job options available to blacks and their traditional employment in those occupations make them dependable sources of labor. Blacks have been preferred mainly for menial and disagreeable occupations but also for some higher-paying occupations such as musicians, athletes, trowel trades in the construction industry, waiters, and longshoremen.

White Workers

As noted earlier, our conceptual model assumes white workers to be primarily motivated by status and job-control considerations in excluding blacks from their jobs. However, whether or not whites succeed in excluding blacks depends on their ability to bring pressure to bear on the employer.

If whites are in sufficient supply to fill particular occupations in the absence of countervailing powers, employers will find it profitable to hire only whites. However, if blacks are in sufficient supply to meet the employer's labor requirements, he might turn to them to weaken white unions. He will not necessarily pay the black workers a different wage, but their presence tends to moderate wage pressures unless blacks and whites form a united bargaining front. Similarly, white workers' bargaining power would be weakened even if blacks were in helper or other mislabeled occupational categories while really performing the same jobs as whites.

Bigoted whites are not likely to quit good jobs because of their racist attitudes, but neither are they likely to demand wage differentials to compensate for their prejudices. Even assuming that they have adequate knowledge of alternatives, prejudiced whites are likely to stay on their jobs if moving is costly in terms of loss of seniority, good wages, and the advantages of specialized, non-transferrable job skills in places where they have worked.

Unions

White workers will use the unions they control to preserve and ration job opportunities. Consequently, the unions do not ordinarily create job discrimination but might be used to perpetuate the exclusion of blacks from certain jobs or to strengthen job segregation within plants.

Race enters union operating procedures in a variety of ways. Different kinds of unions have different motives, procedures, and control mechanisms and therefore will react differently to the presence of black workers in an industry or trade. Unions are motivated by job-control and status considerations to keep blacks out.

Whether or not these unions are able to bar minorities depends mainly on their control of entry into the occupation. Craft unions, for example, ordinarily have considerable control of the supply of labor. The main job-control instruments of craft unions are control of training, entry into the trade and union, and job referrals. In order for blacks to penetrate these crafts and unions, they must ordinarily either threaten the unions' control instruments or inflict monetary losses on unions.

Industrial unions generally have adopted different procedures, mainly because they confront different situations, not because their members had any more or less racial prejudice than craft workers, although job status considerations seem to have been weaker in the case of industrial unions. But the main difference between craft and industrial unions is that the latter have little direct influence over hiring.

In order to organize their jurisdictions, industrial unions must therefore appeal to the workers hired by the employer. Thus, if blacks have been hired in competition with white workers, the union's ability to organize and its bargaining strength will depend on its ability to attract blacks.

Union racial practices also are influenced by union structure. Since federations and national unions have broader political objectives than the locals, the motive for racial equality increases as we move from the local to the national level. Moreover, national craft unions also have stronger motives to take in blacks than their locals, because the national's power depends to some extent upon the size of its membership, whereas the local often conceives its power to depend more narrowly on control of labor supplies in local labor markets.

Blacks

The blacks outside craft unions derive their power mainly from the extent to which they can threaten the wage rates and job-control procedures of discriminating white union members and their leaders; this in turn depends primarily on the number of blacks in a labor market who possess the necessary skills to compete with white union members and secondarily on the extent to which the black community and antidiscriminatory forces are organized to overcome white resistance to the admission of blacks.

Even if civil-rights forces are well organized to achieve this objective, they will have limited impact unless they produce black applicants for employment, upgrading, apprenticeship, and/or journeyman status who meet the qualifications imposed by unions and employers or unless they successfully challenge the standards and specifications themselves. These considerations make it obvious that an effective strategy to overcome local union resistance ordinarily will require considerable attention to local labor-market conditions and the control mechanisms used by the local union to regulate labor supplies and to control jobs.

Environmental Factors

These specific and immediate forces affecting black employment patterns are influenced by such environmental factors as the relative amount and quality of education available to blacks, race relations in the larger community, the age and sex composition of the black work force, alternative income sources available to black workers and their families, housing patterns and transportation costs relative to the location of jobs, the physical and emotional health of blacks relative to whites, whether an industry is growing or declining in terms of employment, black and white migration patterns, the structure of the industry in terms of its customers (blacks, whites, other employees, or government), general business conditions, skill requirements and job structures within industry, the black community's relative accessibility to job information, and the processes through which employers and unions recruit and train workers for jobs.

Although all of these factors are important determinants of black employment patterns, some are more important and measurable than others. General business conditions are very important, because tight labor markets facilitate the employment and upgrading of blacks. However, this view must be qualified, because experience makes it clear that tight labor markets are not sufficient causes of change. Many cities which enjoyed low official unemployment rates during the 1960s also had stable racial employment patterns between 1920 and the 1960s.

Moreover, there is a difference between a labor market where unemployment is declining and one where unemployment is low and stable. Similarly, the overall unemployment rate obscures particular labor-market conditions which prevent blacks from obtaining jobs. Finally, concerted efforts to change institutional arrangements can make it possible for black employment to increase in a particular category even when white employment is falling.

The systems model has some policy implications which are similar to those of the neoclassical model. The neoclassicists are correct in stressing measures to increase black productivity as a means of improving their economic position. But they are wrong in assuming that competitive forces alone will gain blacks access to the jobs for which they qualify themselves.

Policies must be undertaken to overcome employer and community opposition and white workers' control of jobs. Indeed, if blacks are unable to gain access to jobs, there is no effective way they can acquire the on-the-job training so essential for access to many better jobs. Black workers certainly are not going to be able to gain access to many of these jobs and on-the-job training opportunities by agreeing to work for lower wages than white incumbents.

The neoclassical model gives no place to group activities in changing employment opportunities, whereas a systems model stresses the need for group action to initiate changes in rules and laws to which individuals adapt.

The systems model also stresses the need to explore the relationships between attitudes, overt and institutional discrimination, and market forces in order to determine how discrimination can be reduced or eliminated.

The policy implications for combating discrimination depend in part on whether we accept the "taste for discrimination" of the neoclassical model or the "perception of reality" formulation. The former would imply measures to reduce discrimination tastes directly or indirectly through competitive forces. The latter would require more accurate labor-market information to cause the probabilities of selecting qualified whites and qualified blacks to converge.

The present study moves from the level of the aggregate to the particular to examine specific cases where enforcement action has been taken. In viewing individual cases—some of which have been effective and some of which have not—it is hoped that insight can be gained not only into whether EEO enforcement works but why it succeeds or fails.

In Chapter 2, attention is focused on five individual court cases which reflect the key issues in integrating the work force of the construction industry: union entry and job referral. Chapter 3 examines the effectiveness of compliance efforts with five major shipyards across the country. In addition to entry to craft jobs, upgrading and seniority systems are key issues in this industry.

NOTES

1. Arvil V. Adams, *Toward Fair Employment and the EEOC: A Study of Compliance Procedures under Title VII of the Civil Rights Act of 1964* (Washington, D.C.: Equal Employment Opportunity Commission, August 31, 1972), pp. 117-22.

2. Equal Employment Opportunity Commission, *Sixth Annual Report* (Washington, D.C.: U.S. Government Printing Office, March 30, 1972), pp. 23-24.

3. Karen E. DeWitt, "Labor Report–EEOC Accelerates Action against Business, Labor Employee Discrimination," *National Journal*, June 23, 1973.

4. Memorandum from Phillip Davis, director, Office of Federal Contract Compliance, May 15, 1975.

5. Maia Licker, "Bringing Equality to the Nation's Steel Mess Is a Long and Bitter Task," *Wall Street Journal*, August 8, 1973, pp. 1, 21.

6. U.S. Department of Labor, Manpower Administration, Office of Manpower, Automation, and Training, *Social and Economic Implications of Integration in the Public Schools*, seminar on manpower policy and program (Washington, D.C.: U.S. Government Printing Office, 1964), p. 6.

7. F. Ray Marshall and Vernon Briggs, Jr., "Remedies for Discrimination in Apprenticeship Programs," *Industrial Relations* 6, no. 3 (May 1967): 306.

8. F. Ray Marshall and Vernon Briggs, Jr., *The Negro and Apprenticeship* (Baltimore: Johns Hopkins University Press, 1967), p. 28.

9. Kenneth B. Clark, "Efficiency as a Prod to Social Action," *Monthly Labor Review* 92, no. 8 (August 1969): 55.

10. Herbert R. Northrup, *The Negro in the Tobacco Industry* (Philadelphia: University of Pennsylvania, 1970), pp. 78-80.

11. *Daily Labor Report*, April 24, 1970, p. A-1.

12. D. L. Hiestand, *Discrimination in Employment: An Appraisal of Research*, Policy Papers in Human Resources and Industrial Relations No. 16 (Ann Arbor: Institute of Labor and Industrial Relations, University of Michigan/Wayne State University, 1970), p. 45.

13. W. M. Landes, "The Effect of State Fair Employment Laws on the Economic Position of Nonwhites," *American Economic Review* 56, no. 2 (1967): 578-90.

14. L. H. Mayhew, *Law and Equal Opportunity: A Study of the Massachusetts Commission against Discrimination* (Cambridge, Mass.: Harvard University Press, 1968), p. 271; J. Minski, "FEPC in Illinois: Four Stormy Years," *Notre Dame Lawyer* 41 (December 1965): 175-76; and P. H. Norgren and S. E. Hill, *Toward Fair Employment* (New York: Columbia University Press, 1964).

15. M. H. Liggett, "The Efficacy of State Fair Employment Practices Commissions," *Industrial and Labor Relations Review* 22 (July 1969): 559-67; Minski, op. cit., pp. 175-76; and Norgren and Hill, op. cit.

16. Adams, op. cit.

17. Ibid., p. 18.

18. Ibid., pp. 106-25.

19. A. Kidder, *Changes in Minority Participation in the Textile Industry of North and South Carolina, 1966 to 1969* (Washington, D.C.: Equal Employment Opportunity Commission, 1972).

20. B. W. Wolkinson, *Unions and the EEOC: A Study of Administrative Futility* (Lexington, Mass.: D. C. Heath, 1973).

21. R. B. Freeman, "Changes in the Labor Market for Black Americans, 1948-72," *Brookings Papers on Economic Activity* (Washington, D.C.: Brookings Institution, January 1973), pp. 67-131; and A. H. Beller, "The Effects of Title VII of the Civil Rights Act of 1964 on the Economic Position of Minorities," Ph.D. dissertation, Columbia University, in process.

22. Freeman, op. cit., p. 119.

23. Allan G. King and F. Ray Marshall, "Black-White Economic Convergence and the Civil Rights Act of 1964," *Labor Law Journal* 25, no. 8 (August 1974): 462-71.

24. Gregory J. Ahart, "A Process Evaluation of the Contract Compliance Program in Nonconstruction Industry," *Industrial and Labor Relations Review* 29, no. 4 (July 1976): 565-71.

25. For example, see U.S. Civil Rights Commission, *Federal Civil Rights Enforcement Effort, 1970* (Washington, D.C.: U.S. Government Printing Office, 1970), and *The Federal Civil Rights Enforcement Effort: One Year Later* (Washington, D.C.: U.S. Government Printing Office, 1971).

26. See Morris Goldstein and Robert S. Smith, "The Estimated Impact of the Antidiscrimination Program Aimed at Federal Contractors," *Industrial Relations Review* 29, no. 4 (July 1976): 523-43; and James J. Heckman and Kenneth I. Wolpin, "Does the Contract Compliance Program Work? An Analysis of Chicago Data," *Industrial Relations Review* 29, no. 4 (July 1976): 544-64.

27. F. Ray Marshall, ed., *Employment of Blacks in the South: A Perspective on the 1960's* (Austin: University of Texas Press, 1978); F. Ray Marshall, *The Negro and Organized Labor* (New York: John Wiley, 1965); Marshall and Briggs, *The Negro and Apprenticeship*, op. cit.; F. Ray Marshall, *The Negro Worker* (New York: Random House, 1967); F. Ray Marshall, "The Economics of Racial Discrimination: A Survey," *Journal of Economic Literature* 12, no. 3 (September 1974): 849-71.

28. John Dunlop, *Industrial Relations Systems* (New York: Henry Holt, 1958).

2

COMBATING EMPLOYMENT DISCRIMINATION IN UNION ENTRY AND JOB REFERRAL THROUGH LITIGATION: THE CASE OF CONSTRUCTION

INTRODUCTION

In the past decade, the construction industry has received more nationwide attention with regard to racial employment discrimination than perhaps any other sector of the economy. There are several reasons why this industry has been singled out for special attention.

First, construction activity is highly visible, since a great deal of the work occurs outdoors. A segregated work force is thus easy to recognize and, especially if the project is in a minority neighborhood, can prove to be an attractive target for individuals who feel that they have been discriminated against.

Second, construction wages are relatively high, and some of the required skills can be learned with a minimum of formal education. A high school diploma with algebra is the maximum formal education required for any construction trade.

Third, a significant share (about 20 percent) of construction is financed either directly or indirectly (through matching grants) by the federal government. Expending federal dollars on projects where discrimination is practiced seems particularly unfair to minorities.

In addition to the above factors, desegregation of the construction industry has taken on a symbolic importance to minorities because of the building trade unions' vigorous resistance to the admission of minorities. As late as 1972, the EEOC reported that although there had been an overall increase in minority membership in construction unions, minority membership in the higher-skilled, better-paying unions had not significantly increased.[1]

Only in isolated cases have demonstrable gains been made in the more prestigious crafts. Employment gains have been primarily in unions with already high minority participation rates (for example, laborers, roofers, trowel trades).

The very fact that so much energy has been expended with so small an apparent gain seems to have strengthened minority resolve to enter these crafts.

The problem of dealing with discrimination against minorities in the construction trades has been complicated because the discrimination, at least in recent years, has been more institutional than overt. Minorities generally have been at a disadvantage in meeting the qualifications for apprenticeship programs, since both the quantity and quality of their formal education are lower than that for otherwise comparable whites.

Moreover, the aspirations of minority youths have been conditioned by the realities that have faced their older peers. Consequently, unions could claim—and be technically correct—that the dearth of minority apprentices was due to the tiny number of applicants. Overt discrimination was unnecessary in such an atmosphere.

Several approaches have been employed to deal with the underrepresentation of minorities in construction unions.

Plans

Two types of plans have been used to encourage the use of minority construction workers "Imposed" plans, such as the controversial Philadelphia plan, have specific federally imposed goals and timetables with respect to minority employment. If the goals and timetables are not met, the relevant unions or contractors are declared in noncompliance and are, theoretically, ineligible to participate in large-scale federal projects unless they can demonstrate that they have made good-faith efforts to meet them.

Penalties for violating the plan run from contract suspension or cancellation to debarment from future work. In practice, this power has seldom been used and then only to delay briefly contract awards.

Imposed plans have been strongly resisted by both unions and contractors, who perceived that they were temporarily successful in avoiding imposed plans by negotiating with the government hometown plans, where the goals and timetables are set by mutual agreement. Minority groups have generally opposed this latter concept, as they have been unwilling to depend on good-faith efforts in a voluntary environment. As a consequence of the limited progress generally made by hometown plans, the Department of Labor has relied increasingly on the use of imposed plans since the early 1970s.

Outreach

Outreach programs are minority-based recruitment and counseling efforts which search minority communities for candidates who can meet the apprenticeship or journeyman standards of the various trades. The organizations sometimes have been associated with an imposed or hometown plan but more often act as independent agencies financed by government or private foundation grants.

Law

Legal sanctions against discrimination in the construction industry have taken two forms: executive action and civil rights law. Since President Franklin D. Roosevelt issued the first executive order during World War II requiring that all federal contractors adopt nondiscriminatory employment practices, federal agencies have required nondiscrimination clauses in contracts with private employers. The Office of Federal Contract Compliance, which promulgated the Philadelphia plan, has had general responsibility for enforcing these contract clauses.

Title VII of the Civil Rights Act of 1964 has resulted in a number of legal decisions and subsequent enforcement activity regarding the employment rights of minorities in the construction trades.

The specific purpose of this section is to assess the extent, if any, to which litigation has been a successful tool in promoting equal employment opportunity in the construction industry. While any progress toward integration of the construction trades involves interaction of *all* of the policy tools used and a myriad of other factors, it is hoped that through close scrutiny of five Title VII lawsuits we can sort out the commonalities of success and failure and make some general conclusions regarding them.

In particular, we wish to address—under varying conditions—the question of whether the litigation was an essential element in the changes in the status of minorities in the construction industry or whether the litigation was inconsequential.

To this end, we turn now to study five cases: *U.S. v. Sheet Metal Workers Local 36* (St. Louis), *Local 53 v. Vogler* (New Orleans), *Dobbins v. Local 212* (Cincinnati), *U.S. v. Ironworkers Local 86* (Seattle), and *U.S. v. Lathers Local 46* (New York).[2] The particular cases studied were selected in consultation with the EEOC and the OFCC and clearly focus on the critical issues in discrimination in the construction industry: entry and job referral.

U.S. V. SHEET METAL WORKERS LOCAL 36
(ST. LOUIS)

Local 36 of the Sheet Metal Workers International Association (SMW) has jurisdiction in St. Louis and 44 counties of eastern Missouri. In 1966 the membership of SMW Local 36 consisted of approximately 1,250 journeymen, all of whom were white, and 110 apprentices, one of whom was black.

The other union involved in this suit, Local 1 of the International Brotherhood of Electrical Workers (IBEW), operates in St. Louis and 24 counties of eastern and southern Missouri. In 1966 there were no blacks in IBEW Local 1 among the approximately 2,000 construction journeymen and apprentices. (The total membership of IBEW Local 1 is about 5,300; the primary source of non-construction employment is the aerospace industry.) In 1966 the St. Louis SMSA* was 36 percent black, with other minority representation negligible.

Both unions were engaged, beginning in 1964, in the construction of the "gateway arch" in downtown St. Louis. This project was supervised by the National Park Service and was intended to dramatize the role of St. Louis as the "gateway to the West."

In 1965 a coalition of minority groups, headed by black civil rights activist Percy Green, began to voice objections concerning the racial composition of the work force on the project. Green pointed out that the construction sites of the arch and that of the adjoining Busch Stadium were in a previously black urban renewal area. Federal action on the composition of the work force was precipitated by a series of protests, culminating in a demonstration during which Green chained himself to the top of the arch.

The Park Service responded to these pressures by requiring each contractor thereafter to employ a minimum percentage of minority workers. When the general contractor subsequently was forced to engage a black-owned non-AFL-CIO plumber's shop—Smith Plumbers, whose workers were affiliated with the Congress of Independent Unions (CIU)—the AFL-CIO workers walked off the job.

The AFL-CIO unions contended that the walkout was due to the presence of non-AFL-CIO workers, but black leaders (particularly Green and Arthur Kennedy of the NAACP†) pointed out that the CIU local was certified by the NLRB and ascribed racial motivation to the work stoppage. At the request of the NAACP, the Department of Justice investigated the situation.

In February 1966 the U.S. attorney general filed a Title VII suit against four of the unions involved in the walkout: IBEW Local 1 and SMW Local 36 plus Plumbers Local 5 and Steamfitters Local 562. This was the first suit filed by the United States under Title VII.

The government alleged that the unions had failed to admit blacks on a nondiscriminatory basis; failed to operate their respective hiring-hall referral systems in a nondiscriminatory manner; failed to inform blacks of opportunities

---

*Standard Metropolitan Statistical Area.
†National Association for the Advancement of Colored People.

to become members; and failed to organize employers who employed blacks. Prior to the trial, the plumbers and the steamfitters signed a consent decree which admitted the substantial points of the government's complaint and committed the unions to remedial action.

The district court denied relief to the United States, finding that although both of the defendants had excluded blacks prior to the effective date of Title VII (July 2, 1965), there were no specific instances of discrimination after that date and that in fact both locals had made postact efforts to recruit blacks.

The court of appeals reversed the district court's findings. The decision held that there was no evidence that either of the locals had changed its pre-1965 discriminatory policies and that such discriminatory policies continued to influence the employment possibilities for blacks after 1965.

In addition to requiring that the unions in the future admit blacks on a nondiscriminatory basis, the relief granted by the court of appeals included the following provisions: the experience requirements of the locals—which required set amounts of time under the collective bargaining agreement before achieving journeyman status—were to be waived in the case of blacks who had gained equivalent experience outside the collective bargaining agreement; reasonable steps were to be taken to make it known to blacks that all persons were permitted to use the referral system without regard to race; and subjective admission standards (for SMW Local 36 only) were to be made more objective so as to permit review. It is noteworthy, however, that the decision contains no specific reference to goals for minority membership. The unions were required only not to discriminate in the future.

The decision against IBEW Local 1 and SMW Local 36 did provide a demonstration effect which caused other St. Louis unions to reevaluate their admission and referral practices. The joint deliberations of these unions and the corresponding contractor associations resulted in the signing of the St. Louis Supplemental Manpower Agreement, or hometown plan, in October 1969. Seven crafts (including Local 36) and their respective trade associations signed the agreement, which projected that minorities were to comprise 20 percent of the work force within five years. (Other crafts were carpenters, operating engineers, concrete masons, roofers, plasterers, and lathers.)

The Joint Administrative Committee of the St. Louis Supplemental Manpower Agreement (funded by the Department of Labor) was established to implement the plan. In the first year of operation, the committee and an additional outreach program run by the Urban League (Project LEAP*) combined to place about 250 minority workers in the trades as either beginning apprentices or trainees (individuals given some advance credit in the apprenticeship program for previously acquired skills).

---

*Labor Education Advancement Program.

The hometown plan, however, contained exact goals for only the carpenters and was elsewhere to be enforced only insofar as it was "consistent with possible fluctuations of industry manpower needs and demands."[3] The plan was rejected on this basis by the Department of Labor. The carpenters were allowed to remain under the hometown plan.

The Department of Labor in July 1971 announced an imposed plan for 16 construction trades and at the same time withdrew the funding of the Joint Administrative Committee. IBEW Local 1 and SMW Local 36 were included and are thus under the jurisdiction of both the court and the imposed plan.

Under the plan, no contracts are awarded for federally involved construction projects exceeding $500,000 unless the bidder agrees to specific minority utilization goals in all work (including nonfederal work). The plan sought an increase of approximately 2,500 minority craft workers in 1976. The acceptable minimums by craft are given in Table 2.1. A 1972 survey of the 16 crafts, however, revealed that only five had minority percentages above the minimums given in Table 2.1. The results of this survey are given in Table 2.2.

The reason most often cited for this continuing underrepresentation of minorities in the building trades is the sluggishness of construction activity in St. Louis. Unions have argued that to admit large numbers of minorities would require the displacement of whites. This sluggishness is evidenced by data given in Table 2.3, which reports the value of building permits issued in the city of St. Louis from 1960 to 1972.

The erratic behavior of construction activity in St. Louis has no doubt made integration of the building trades more difficult. It might in fact be argued for the unions that the increase in minority employment accomplished in the face of a decreasing demand for construction workers actually understates the net gains to minorities, since minority employment has in the past typically decreased absolutely as unemployment rises.

Still, under the law, neither of these arguments is a sufficient excuse for the plan's failure to meet its goals. Title VII requires not that jobs be available but only that minorities be given equal access to the jobs which are available.

Another apparent reason why the St. Louis plan has failed to meet its goals is the seeming indifference of the parties concerned toward its enforcement. For example, no minority organization has maintained the steady pressure which might have forced compliance. The two local outreach agencies, Project LEAP and the Joint Administrative Committee, owed their existence primarily to the defunct hometown plan and were, as a result, understaffed and underfunded. The nearest Office of Federal Contract Compliance representative, who is technically in charge of monitoring the plan, is in Kansas City. The U.S. attorney's office refers any complaints to Washington, D.C.

The status of minorities in the St. Louis building trades has thus improved, but this progress has fallen well short of even the most modest expectations outlined in Table 2.1. With this result, can any assessment be made of the net impact of *U.S. v. Sheet Metal Workers Local 36*?

TABLE 2.1

Imposed Minimum Minority Representation, 1971–75
(percentages)

Craft	1971	1972	1973	1974	1975
Asbestos workers	3.2	3.7	4.2	4.7	5.2
Boilermakers	20.2	23.9	26.6	30.3	34.0
Bricklayers	6.2	7.8	9.4	11.0	12.6
Carpenters	2.2	3.7	5.2	7.7	8.2
Cement workers	4.1	6.4	8.7	11.0	13.3
Electricians	3.4	6.9	8.5	11.1	13.6
Elevator constructors	2.5	4.1	5.6	7.2	8.7
Glaziers	5.7	11.5	17.2	23.0	28.7
Ironworkers	3.4	4.8	6.2	7.6	9.0
Lathers	6.2	10.7	15.2	19.7	24.2
Operating engineers	3.2	5.7	8.2	16.7	13.2
Painters and paperhangers	6.1	10.9	15.6	20.4	25.1
Plumbers and pipefitters	4.0	6.2	8.4	10.6	13.2
Roofers	7.1	9.6	12.1	14.6	17.1
Sheet metal workers	4.5	9.0	13.5	18.0	22.5
Tile setters	2.4	4.0	5.6	7.2	8.8

Source: Department of Labor News Release dated July 7, 1971.

TABLE 2.2

Minority Representation in the St. Louis Construction Trades, 1972

Craft	Active* Membership	Minority Journeymen	Minority Apprentices	Minority Trainees	Percent Minorities	1972 Minimum Percent
Asbestos workers	300	0	5	0	1.6	3.7
Boilermakers	56	0	3	0	5.4	23.9
Bricklayers	1,000	69	1	3	7.3	7.8
Carpenters	3,210	471	44	55	17.8	3.7
Cement workers	431	27	9	10	10.7	6.4
Electricians	1,600	46	20	20	5.4	6.9
Elevator constructors	212	2	6	0	3.8	4.1
Glaziers	182	1	2	0	1.6	11.5
Ironworkers	700	10	10	20	5.7	4.8
Lathers	239	4	2	0	2.5	10.7
Operating engineers	800	71	15	13	12.4	5.7
Painters and paperhangers	1,352	82	22	0	7.7	10.9
Plumbers and pipefitters	2,186	66	28	15	5.0	6.2
Roofers	420	18	19	4	9.8	9.6
Sheet metal workers	650	2	15	25	6.5	9.0
Tile setters	115	1	1	0	1.7	4.0
Total	13,453	870	202	165	9.2	

*An active member is defined as an individual who has worked or applied for work at the hall in the last three months.
Source: Confidential survey.

TABLE 2.3

Value of Building Permits Issued in the City of St. Louis, 1960–72
(in current dollars)

Year	Valuation
1960	$48,661,702
1961	77,091,372
1962	66,176,923
1963	67,246,719
1964	124,012,424
1965	69,322,546
1966	126,062,507
1967	99,364,322
1968	100,315,225
1969	95,032,325
1970	77,752,879
1971	54,485,996
1972	78,144,561

Source: Building Permits Department, City of St. Louis.

The litigation was clearly an important motivating factor in the creation of the St. Louis hometown plan, but it must be recalled that this effort was judged insufficient by the Department of Labor. The imposed plan which followed probably would have come into being whether or not the court case (or the hometown plan) had ever existed.

Since enforcement of the court order has, for all practical purposes, been dominated by the enforcement activities of the imposed plan, we are forced to conclude that the court's decision was coopted by a relatively ineffectual plan which it had no significant role in bringing about. The net impact of the court case has thus been negligible.

LOCAL 53 V. VOGLER
(NEW ORLEANS)

Local 53 of the International Association of Heat and Frost Insulators and Asbestos Workers represents insulation and asbestos workers in southeastern Louisiana (including New Orleans and Baton Rouge) and western Mississippi. Local 53 effectively controls employment and training opportunities in this area through its exclusive bargaining agreements with all major firms doing insulation and asbestos work.

In 1966 there were approximately 1,200 workers employed under the auspices of Local 53. Of these, only 282 were actually union members, including 64 improvers (apprentices). The remaining workers were permit workers or transfers from sister locals. None of the 1,200 workers was black or Mexican-American. Within the jurisdiction of Local 53, over 45 percent of the male work force between ages 18 and 30 was black.[4]

In order to be referred to an insulation or asbestos job, workers were required to sign registers at the union hall. Union members were assigned to different priority groups based upon experience in the trade and residence in the area. The order of referral within these priority groups was determined chronologically.

Once all of the union members were employed, permit holders were referred. The permit workers included members of other trade unions, such as Plasterers Local 93, who were qualified to perform the tasks of an insulation or asbestos mechanic (journeyman).

It was the policy of Local 53 to restrict its membership to sons or close relatives of its members. To become a member, an applicant had to obtain written recommendations from three members and had to be approved by a majority of the members voting by secret ballot. In the four years preceding 1966, Local 53 had accepted 72 improvers; 69 were sons of members, and three were nephews of members who had raised them. The local did not admit new mechanics who had not been improvers, regardless of their qualifications.

In 1966, Paul Vogler, a white nonunion asbestos worker, filed a complaint with the New Orleans office of the EEOC against Local 53 and a New Orleans contractor, McCarty, Inc. Vogler alleged that he was refused employment because of his nonunion status and because of his efforts to assist a black friend, Cashmiere Joseph, to attain union membership.

The EEOC investigated the complaint and found reasonable cause to believe that the charges were true. The EEOC then attempted to conciliate the parties, failed, and referred the case to the Department of Justice.

In December 1966, a Title VII suit was brought against McCarty, Inc., and Local 53. The complaint against McCarty, Inc., was dismissed by the district court, which ruled that the contractor could not hire blacks because of its exclusive bargaining agreement with Local 53.

However, the court also found that Local 53 had engaged in discrimination against blacks, and it issued an injunction against the union (later upheld by the Fifth Circuit Court of Appeals) which prohibited discrimination in excluding persons from union membership or referring persons for work; prohibited use of members' endorsements, family relationship, or elections as criteria for membership; ordered that four individuals be admitted to membership and that nine others be referred for work; ordered the development of objective membership criteria and prohibited new members other than the four until developed; and ordered continuation of chronological referrals for work, with alternating white and black referrals until objective membership criteria were developed.[5]

The court further required that Local 53 increase its membership to 390 and its number of improvers to 130. The local was required immediately to admit 44 specifically named blacks (including Joseph) as mechanics and 55 blacks as improvers. If any of the specifically named blacks refused the offer to become mechanics, another black would be substituted by the court. All improvers with at least 4,800 hours of experience were to be promoted to mechanic status. The effect of the decree was to boost membership to 520. Of these members, 99 were black.

In order to fulfill the injunction's requirement that blacks and whites be referred alternately, Local 53 was instructed to maintain different work registers for blacks and whites. The decree specified that the work registers for each race were to be broken down based upon experience. There were to be two categories: the first to consist of workers with more than five 1,200-hour years of experience in the insulation or asbestos trade and the second to consist of workers with less than five years of such experience. Preference for referrals would be given to those in the first category.

The union, however, was eventually allowed to establish a different system inasmuch as very few of the blacks had five years' experience. In the revised system, the register for blacks was broken into two categories; those with at least 500 hours of work were listed in the "A" register.

The register for white workers was then divided into three categories. Those workers with five years and at least 4,800 hours of work were listed in the "A" register; those with less than five years but at least 4,800 hours of work were listed in the "B" register; those with less than five years or 4,800 hours were placed in the "C" register. Assignment from a register was based upon chronological order in the register.

Membership in Local 53 since 1968 has remained approximately constant at 520 members, with 99 of the members black, as required by the decree. The local has, however, experienced a high rate of turnover in its black membership. By late 1974, fewer than one-fourth of the original 44 black mechanics remained in the local.

It has been widely alleged that the high number of quits among blacks has been due to a combination of inadequate training opportunities, inferior job assignments, and harassment on the job. But none of these charges has ever been substantiated and brought before the court, despite the fact that such practices are clearly unlawful.

Local 53 v. Vogler has provided a demonstration effect which has induced other New Orleans construction trades to participate in a hometown plan. The New Orleans (hometown) plan was funded by the Department of Labor in 1971. The plan's main purpose is to provide qualified minority applicants so that its goal of attaining at least 20 percent minority representation in each signatory craft by 1976 can be reached. The 20 percent goal is based on minority work force representation in the New Orleans parish (county).

TABLE 2.4

Minority Representation and Goals for Nonexempt Locals, New Orleans
(goals and figures are as of October 1974)

Craft	Goals	Minorities	Percent of Goal
Boilermakers	40	20	50.0
Carpenters	101	72	71.3
Electricians	163	155	95.1
Elevator constructors	36	22	61.1
Glaziers	12	11	91.7
Ironworkers	100	69	69.0
Operating engineers	152	124	81.6
Painters	110	89	80.9
Pile drivers	43	32	74.4
Plumbers	150	148	98.7
Sheet metal workers	75	63	84.0
Total	982	805	82.0

Source: New Orleans Plan Administrative Committee Monthly Survey Report.

The plan's director, Lambert Boissiere, has been active in attempting to force recalcitrant unions to sign the plan and to comply with its goals. At his behest, three New Orleans construction locals—the sheet metal workers, the electricians, and the plumbers—were charged in 1973 with Title VII violations by the Department of Justice. Although all three cases were settled before trial, the three locals are now effectively under the control of the hometown plan. By 1975, 22 crafts with New Orleans jurisdiction had signed the hometown plan.

As the results given in Table 2.4 indicate, none of the 11 locals which had less than 20 percent minority membership at the time they signed the plan (nonexempt locals) had met its established goals by October 1974. Several of the unions were, however, near their goals, and the total percentage effort (82 percent) was impressive.

Boissiere and other minority leaders in New Orleans credit the progress which has been made to the continued threat of legal sanctions against the construction unions and make a strong case that the initial prosecution of *Local 53 v. Vogler* was necessary to make this threat real. Thus, the Vogler case has apparently provided a strong positive impetus to equal employment opportunity in New Orleans.

DOBBINS V. LOCAL 212
(CINCINNATI)

In January 1966, Anderson L. Dobbins, a black, filed a complaint with the EEOC against IBEW Local 212. Dobbins charged that the local had refused to admit qualified blacks, specifically Dobbins himself, to membership.

The jurisdiction of IBEW Local 212 includes Cincinnati and 13 adjoining counties of Ohio, Kentucky, and Indiana. Prior to 1968, the membership policies of the local were governed by its collective bargaining agreement, the constitution of the international, and its own bylaws.

There were two methods of becoming a union member. One path was to go through the regular apprenticeship program; the other was to work for four years in the trade for either a union or a nonunion contractor. In the latter case, an examination was required before certification as a journeyman was granted.

Although the bylaws required the union's examining board to meet at least once monthly when there were applicants to be examined, the board met infrequently. There were no meetings between 1963 and 1968. This was true despite the fact that there were at all times applicants for membership and that the union's membership was consistently lower than the number of electricians needed.

IBEW Local 212 had a membership in 1966 of 770 white males; it had never had a black member. Between 1960 and 1966, 18 blacks applied for membership, and nine of these made application after the effective date of Title VII. In addition, although according to the collective bargaining agreement all employees of union contractors were required to become and remain members of the union from and after the thirty-first day of employment, the union did not enforce this provision. Consequently, there were nonunion referrals. No blacks were referred prior to 1967.

In February 1967 the EEOC ruled that reasonable cause existed to believe that IBEW Local 212 was in violation of Title VII. Subsequent attempts to reach a voluntary settlement with the union were unsuccessful, and in May 1967, Dobbins—assisted by the local chapter of the NAACP—filed a Title VII suit against the electricians. In July 1967 the Department of Justice brought a separate action against IBEW Local 212, claiming general discrimination with respect to membership and employment opportunities. In September 1967, on the motion of the United States, the two actions were consolidated. In April 1968 the Cincinnati Electrical Joint Apprenticeship and Training Committee was added as a defendant.

The major findings of the court in its judgment of September 1968 and orders of October 1968 were threefold. First, the court found that the union's testing procedures bore no rational relationship to the qualifications of individuals for the trade and that the direct journeyman examination was administered too infrequently.

The union was ordered not to administer examinations which were not reasonably related to the skills required in the everyday work of a construction electrician. The direct examination was to be conducted at least every three months. The union was further ordered to admit Dobbins immediately to full membership and to admit to membership other blacks, providing they passed an examination for journeyman electricians administered by the Northern Kentucky Electrical Authority.

Second, the court found that the union's exclusive hiring-hall agreement was not discriminatory per se but that the referral system as written into the collective bargaining agreement provided no guidelines for its actual application. The court provided specific guidelines which guarded against further racial discrimination in job referral.

Third, the court found that the Joint Apprenticeship and Training Committee had failed to accept the evaluations of applicants by its own hired experts (transcript evaluation and aptitude) and had fairly consistently given preference to whites (especially relatives of members) over blacks. The committee was enjoined against this practice.

The impact of the Dobbins decision on equal employment opportunity in Cincinnati should be considered as a marginal but nevertheless important factor in the broader efforts to desegregate the Cincinnati building trades. The city of Cincinnati in 1960 was 27.5 percent black, and the SMSA was 12 percent black (blacks constituting the only significant minority group).

Employment opportunities in most of the skilled building trades, however, were open only to whites. Although precise data on the number of minorities in the trades in the early 1960s are not available, a 1952 report to the Cincinnati City Council accurately reflected a situation which held true as late as 1963:

> Within the unionized construction field, Negroes are found exclusively (or with purely negligible exception) only on common labor jobs, skilled jobs being white only. The Hod-Carriers and Building Laborers Union has about 75 percent Negro membership. On the other hand, the Carpenters, Bricklayers, Plasterers, Painters, Electricians, Plumbers, and Steamfitters are exclusively (or with negligible exception) white.[6]

The first serious challenge to these segregated conditions came in the summer of 1963, when the local chapters of the Congress of Racial Equality and the NAACP demonstrated against the composition of the work force at the new downtown federal building. Over the next two years, desegregation efforts were extended to such employers as Procter and Gamble, the Cincinnati *Post*, and the First National Bank.

But in 1965, at the urging of Herbert Hill, national labor secretary for the NAACP, attention was refocused on the construction trades. Hill reasoned that the diffusion of effort across all employment was counterproductive and that construction, due to the large amount of federal funding involved, made a particularly attractive target.

The result was a flurry of demonstrations that led to a manpower program funded by the Department of Labor, the Journeyman Union Manpower Program (JUMP). The purpose of the program was to upgrade to journeyman status semi-skilled blacks recruited by a city governmental agency, the Cincinnati Human Relations Commission.

This program failed to make significant progress in increasing black membership in the building trade unions. Black leaders claimed that the failure was due to union intransigence. Union leaders claimed that the referrals from JUMP were not trainable and that the JUMP staff was not knowledgeable about the construction industry.

By 1968, demonstrations had resumed, with attention focusing on the city's new sports complex, Riverfront Stadium, which was being constructed on an urban renewal site. The Dobbins case was contemporaneous with these demonstrations.

A coalition of concerned parties from the trade unions, the contractor associations, and the black community was formed at this time, and the result of their deliberations was what has become known as the Cincinnati plan. Before discussing the specifics of the plan or its effectiveness, however, it is worthwhile to speculate on the motives which, if nothing else, brought these diverse economic actors to an agreement which has lasted for over six years.

The unions and the contractor associations were apparently motivated by the same factors. First, they had been subject to sustained demonstrations and charges of racism for over five years. The demonstration pressures were not, as they once might have hoped, lessening. The resultant financial losses and adverse publicity no doubt helped convince the unions and the contractors that some sort of reconciliation with the NAACP was desirable.

Second, pressure for union desegregation from the government both in the form of direct court intervention (the Dobbins case) and of contract compliance action was mounting. The unions and the contractors were upset over what they considered to be intervention by public officials (judges and government bureaucrats) who had little or no understanding of the construction industry. For example, there was great fear that either a court or the OFCC would impose a plan for black employment which would lower work and training standards. Additionally, there was fear that financial losses could result from either court fines or contract compliance sanctions.

As important as the change in the bargaining position of the union/contractor side was the continued presence of recognized black leaders (particularly Lucy Green of the NAACP) at the negotiations. Perhaps because of their own fatigue from having engaged in desegregation demonstrations almost continuously for five years and a feeling that the impact of such demonstrations was beginning to fade, these representatives endured a sometimes bitter debate within the local NAACP chapter over the negotiations and gave the eventual settlement credence in the black community.

The failure of the JUMP program and the resulting consultations with Ray Marshall (then of the University of Kentucky and coauthor of the book *The Negro and Apprenticeship*)[7] and Department of Labor personnel convinced the coalition that any new program must contain a strong outreach and training component.

In October 1968 the Department of Labor funded the Preparation Recruitment Employment Program (PREP). PREP is an outreach program which searches the black community for young people who may qualify as apprentices. The program administrators admittedly "cream" in order to find minorities who will have a good chance of meeting union standards. The individuals are given special classes to prepare them for particular apprenticeship examinations. If successful, the individuals enter the regular craft apprenticeship programs.

PREP was augmented in April 1971 by the Journeyman Employment Training (JET) program. The JET program is designed for applicants who are beyond the regular apprenticeable age. Individuals are evaluated as to their experience level and are placed as trainees at the appropriate level of what is effectively the apprenticeship program. Some individuals are placed directly as journeymen.

Evaluation of placement level is made by a committee composed of representatives of the contractors and the unions, one of whom must be black. An attempt is made to tailor the remainder of the training program to an individual's particular skill deficiencies.

The PREP/JET program has become known as the Cincinnati (hometown) plan and has been accepted by the Department of Labor as meeting contract compliance standards. Seventeen building trade crafts are signatories. Local 212 is both signatory to the plan and remains under the jurisdiction of the court from the Dobbins case. (This was accomplished only after Local 212 was ordered by the court to sign the plan. The electricians had originally refused to sign, as the plan is apparently more of a binding constraint than the court order.)

The Cincinnati plan seeks to raise the percentage representation of minorities in each of the crafts to at least 11 percent—slightly less than the percentage of blacks in the Cincinnati SMSA—in the five years from 1971 to 1976. Each craft was allowed to set its own intermediate goals in attaining the 11 percent standard.

Six of the 17 trades have met or exceeded their goals for 1974 (see Table 2.5). The overall percentage representation of minorities (8.1 percent) is heavily influenced by the black-dominated cement masons' union; without the cement masons, the percentage of minorities falls to a less-respectable 5.1 percent.

Two reasons are most often cited for this shortfall. The unions note that the gains which have been made were accomplished during a sharp drop in construction activity during 1972 and 1973. From a peak of $182 million in 1971,

TABLE 2.5

Minority Representation in the Building Trades Covered by the Cincinnati Plan, October 1974

Craft	Membership	Minority Members	Percent Minority	Goal
Asbestos workers	182	8	4.4	17
Boilermakers	333	25	7.5	16
Bricklayers	122	11	9.0	12
Carpenters	2,976	122	4.1	208
Cement masons	457	320	70.0	20
Electricians	841	53	6.3	53
Elevator constructors	298	14	4.7	22
Floor layers	333	11	3.3	16
Glaziers	114	5	4.4	10
Lathers	96	7	7.3	6
Marble workers	91	4	4.4	8
Millwrights	467	14	3.0	17
Painters	822	37	4.5	53
Pipefitters	855	47	5.5	74
Plumbers	610	25	4.1	6
Sheet metal workers	663	55	8.3	47
Operating engineers	700	49	7.0	49
Total	9,960	807	8.1	634

Source: October 1974 survey by PREP-JET.

construction volume dropped to $113 million in 1972 and $134 million in 1973. Table 2.6 reports construction activity in Cincinnati since 1966, the year the Dobbins case was initiated.

The sluggishness of construction activity is, however, as previously noted, no excuse for the shortfalls of the plan. Responsibility for the deficiencies of the plan must ultimately rest with the OFCC, which—although it has repeatedly noted the noncompliance of certain crafts—has yet to use its power to withhold funds. The OFCC may feel that the Cincinnati crafts have made a good-faith effort and that overt action might cause the unions to become intransigent, leading in the end to a counterproductive result.

The progress which has been made by the Cincinnati plan must be attributed primarily to aggressive action by Dobbins and black community groups, such as the NAACP and PREP/JET. Although the direct effect of the Dobbins case is minimal, since its role with respect to the electrical workers has been effectively usurped by the Cincinnati plan and since Dobbins himself no longer works as an electrician, the threat of further overt public intervention resulting

TABLE 2.6

Construction Activity in the City of Cincinnati, 1966–73
(current dollars)

Year	Total Estimated Construction
1966	$114,572,160
1967	119,158,200
1968	140,778,820
1969	114,317,340
1970	101,322,765
1971	182,873,975
1972	113,389,070
1973	134,543,540

Source: Annual reports of the Cincinnati Department of Public Works.

from minority grievances does appear to be the principal motivating factor behind continued progress. Given the statistics in Table 2.5, we are forced to conclude that further aggressive action on the part of minorities will be required to move the Cincinnati plan forward.

U.S. V. IRONWORKERS LOCAL 86
(SEATTLE)

The five Seattle unions originally charged in this suit were Ironworkers Local 86, Sheet Metal Workers Local 99, Plumbers and Pipefitters Local 32, IBEW Local 46, and Operating Engineers Local 302. These locals have jurisdiction, with minor geographical variations, in Seattle and the surrounding area of western Washington.

The number of black journeymen in each local at the time of the trial (February 1970) is shown in Table 2.7. In 1970 the city of Seattle was 7.1 percent black.

The first demonstrations protesting the racial composition of Seattle's construction unions occurred in the early fall of 1969. The protests were led by Tyree Scott, a black electrician who with his father ran a small electrical shop. Scott had recently joined several other minority contractors to form the Central Contractors Association (CCA). The CCA was concerned about the lack of opportunity for blacks in the construction trades.

In August 1969 the group shut down a number of construction sites in both black neighborhoods and downtown Seattle. An agreement was subsequently reached between the CCA and the affected prime contractors requiring that minority trainees be employed on the projects, but implementation of the

TABLE 2.7

Black Journeymen in Five Seattle Unions, February 1970

Union	Number of Journeymen*	Black Journeymen
Ironworkers	920	1
Sheet metal workers	900	1
Plumbers and pipefitters	1,900	1
Electricians	1,750	2
Operating engineers	600	5

*All figures are approximate. The figures for the sheet metal workers and the plumbers and pipefitters include only their construction divisions.
Source: 8618 W. D. Washington 1970.

agreement was blocked when the regular union members walked off the jobs in protest.

The union members were ordered back to work by William J. Lindberg, a federal district judge, who found that the walkout was not due to a legitimate labor dispute. Judge Lindberg also ordered 60 black trainees put to work immediately on five separate construction sites. The wages of the black workers were to be paid by Seattle's Model Cities grant. The program, however, was short-lived, as the blacks—once on the job—were given no work assignments by the project foremen. Within a week, all of the trainees had quit. They were not replaced.

The CCA renewed demonstrations in November 1969, and shutdowns of construction sites at both the University of Washington and Seattle-Tacoma Airport ensued. Because of pressure principally from the construction contractors, who were anxious for financial reasons to halt the frequent work stoppages, the Department of Justice filed a Title VII suit against the five unions mentioned above and their respective Joint Apprenticeship Committees (JACs).

The action alleged that the parties were discriminating against blacks in both admission and job referral. Specific examples were cited where each of the locals and the JACs had discriminated against blacks. The allegations brought against Ironworkers Local 86 and its JAC are illustrative of the evidence presented in the case.

The United States argued that Howard Lewis and Jettie Murray, both experienced black welders of journeyman capability, were denied referral and membership by Local 86 on account of race. In 1962 Lewis obtained an application for membership but could not find two sponsors. In 1966 he made two additional attempts to join. First he was refused because he had not completed the required paper work. Then he was failed on a knot-tying test. Lewis joined the union only in 1969, when the Washington State Board against Discrimination ordered Local 86 to accept him.

Murray applied for referral in 1966 after having been advised that there was a need for welders in the ironworkers' trade. He applied to the union on a regular basis for three months and was told that there was no work. Murray contacted an employer directly and upon instructions went to the union hall for dispatch back to the employer as per the collective bargaining agreement. The business agent of Local 86 refused to dispatch him. The Washington State Board also found discrimination in this case.

It was additionally alleged that in 1969 two black permit holders, Cornelius Bradford and William Bracy, were discriminated against in job referral. Two white permit holders who had signed the work list after the blacks were told that on the payment of a sum of money they would be referred out to work. Bradford and Bracy were not given such an offer.

The government charged the ironworkers' JAC with using aptitude tests which discriminated against blacks. Prior to 1967, applicants were not required to take the exams. When the test was first used, no minimum score was announced. In 1968 the JAC published minimum scores after a pledge of nondiscrimination was made to the Washington State Board. Since the minimum scores were established, approximately 27 percent of the blacks taking the test had passed, while approximately 72 percent of others taking the test had passed.

The decision of the United States to charge these five particular unions was made for two main reasons. First, the unions were large from a membership standpoint (a total of over 6,000 journeymen). The federal government realized that in order to produce witnesses who would attest to specific instances of discrimination, they would have to confront the larger unions. This was also the reason why evidence of discrimination only against blacks was given. Although there was discrimination against other racial groups as well, the U.S. attorney found specific instances difficult to substantiate. (This has subsequently caused some discontent among nonblack Seattle minorities. These other minorities and the construction unions not covered in the Ironworkers Local 86 decision are covered by the Seattle-King County hometown plan.)

Second, the locals were prestigious (relative to other construction crafts) and paid high wages. Other less-prestigious and lower-paying construction trades (for example, roofers, laborers) had long employed substantial numbers of blacks. The government wanted to penetrate the top of the construction profession.

Operating Engineers Local 302 signed a consent decree before the trial date. The local's leadership apparently felt that the case for discrimination was strong and that it would be less costly in the long run to enter into a voluntary agreement. The union admitted the substantive points of the government's complaint and committed itself to corrective action. Specifically, the union agreed to admit 50 minority apprentices for the following three years. The "operating engineers plan," which was to recruit minority candidates and monitor their training, was subsequently funded by the Department of Labor.

The federal district court, with Judge Lindberg presiding, found in June 1970 that the remaining four locals and three JACs (the electricians' JAC was acquitted) were guilty of pursuing a pattern and practice of conduct with respect to employment which had denied to blacks because of their race the same opportunities made available to whites. At the time the judgment was made, Judge Lindberg asked the defendants and the plaintiff to submit proposed remedies.

The court's order was issued less than two weeks later and was largely a product of the proposed remedy submitted by the Department of Justice. The most striking feature of the order is the detail in which the relief is spelled out. The judge apparently agreed with the plaintiff's position that in order to address not only the overt but also the institutional aspects of discrimination, a great deal of specificity was required.

Both a general remedy and a remedy specific to each defendant were provided. The general provisions were:

The defendants were enjoined from discriminating against any person because of race with respect to acquisition or retention of membership or with respect to referral for employment.

The defendants were required to implement a comprehensive record-keeping system which was to include racial and other background data on all applicants for either referral or admission to the union. The defendants were required to transmit these records to the plaintiff quarterly. The plaintiff would then report to the court.

The defendants were required to initiate a program to disseminate information to the black community regarding employment opportunities in their respective trades.

The defendant JACs were ordered to select and indenture a sufficient number of blacks to ensure a level of black participation which would overcome the present effects of past discrimination. The court provided guidelines for each craft.

The defendant JACs were required to implement "special apprenticeship programs" emphasizing on-the-job training to meet the special needs of blacks, with or without experience in the trade, who were too old for the regular apprenticeship programs. A Court Order Advisory Committee (COAC) was established to implement the program. The COAC was to include representatives from labor, the contractor associations, the minority community, and interested governmental agencies.[8]

Again, the remedy relating only to Ironworkers Local 86 and the ironworkers' JAC is illustrative of the specific remedies applied to each of the defendants. The main provisions of the ironworkers remedy were:

Local 86 was required to offer journeyman membership to black iron-workers with over 700 hours of experience upon payment of the standard initiation fees.

Local 86 was henceforth required to refer individuals for employment on the basis of the order in which they signed the work list in their particular priority grouping. The union could not require an examination on previous experience under the collective bargaining agreement as a prerequisite to the placement of a black applicant's name on the work list. Because black journeymen had generally been denied the opportunity to acquire work experience, the court ordered that they could be called for work by contractors irrespective of their place on the work list.

The union was ordered to provide immediate referrals and applications for membership to a list of individuals who had been the victims of discrimination.

The ironworkers' JAC was ordered to discontinue the use of culturally biased aptitude tests and was ordered to admit to its regular or special apprenticeship program six individuals who had been the victims of discrimination.

The degree to which the court order has subsequently been implemented has been largely a matter of resolving conflicts which have frequently arisen between the parties affected by the decision. The principal adversaries have been the black community and the defendant unions, with the principal forum for debate the COAC. Judge Lindberg has acted through the use of both supplemental orders and persuasion as a powerful third force in these discussions.

The first confrontation occurred only three months after the original order. While the decision was under appeal to the federal circuit court (the decision was eventually upheld), the defendants were reluctant to take more than minimal action. In addition, for some time the defendants harbored hopes of replacing the court order with participation in the Seattle hometown plan. The COAC members originally appointed from the minority community were moderate and were unwilling to force issues in that forum actively.

Tyree Scott had by this time split off from the CCA over worker/management issues and had formed, with the assistance of the American Friends Service Committee, the United Construction Workers Association (UCWA). The UCWA began demonstrations against the nonenforcement of the order in September 1970.

Judge Lindberg (reportedly furious) reacted with a supplemental order which gave the unions ten days to indenture the required number of apprentices. Ninety blacks were in fact recruited by the UCWA and admitted to the apprenticeship program. Few of these individuals, however, remained on the job, since—as both the UCWA and the unions admit—no standards were set for their selection.

TABLE 2.8

Population and Employment in the Seattle SMSA, 1970-73

Year	Population	Civilian Labor Force	Employment	Unemployment Rate
1970	1,424,611	640,500	579,000	9.5
1971	1,432,800	633,900	550,900	13.0
1972	1,411,900	630,500	567,400	9.9
1973	1,409,400	644,200	595,400	7.6

Source: Employment Security Department, State of Washington, *Annual Manpower Planning Report 1974*, Seattle-Everett Washington Area.

The UCWA subsequently requested that the COAC retain the UCWA to assist in recruiting and counseling. After initially approving the plan, the COAC reversed itself, citing as the principal reasons the militancy of the UCWA and the threat of dual unionism. The minority representatives then walked off the committee, and the chairman, Donald Close of the National Electrical Contractors Association, resigned. Close had voted with the majority and cited lack of confidence in him by the black community as the reason for his resignation.

Judge Lindberg issued another supplemental order, altering the role of the COAC. The order provided for a nonvoting, impartial chairperson in addition to the other members and directed the COAC to monitor the special apprentices more actively. Professor Luvern V. Rieke of the University of Washington Law School was named chairperson. The judge still refused to allow the UCWA any formal role in the implementation of the original or supplemental orders.

Still, there were only negligible increases in black participation in the defendant unions. Despite its specificity elsewhere, the original court order had not provided timetables against which compliance could be assessed. Furthermore, economic activity in general and construction activity in particular began to decline in Seattle in 1971. Employment dropped sharply during the so-called Boeing recession and did not recover above the 1970 level until 1973 (see Table 2.8).

The defendant unions thus argued that to provide equal employment opportunities to blacks would mean displacing whites. The unions made this argument despite the fact that they continued to indenture white apprentices. Furthermore, since the U.S. attorney's office in Seattle had no one with full-time responsibility for monitoring the order, quarterly reports from the defendants often were not filed.

In order to facilitate the placement of additional minority apprentices, the COAC in early 1972 recommended that the court amend, by decree, the collective bargaining agreements of the defendant unions so that instead of allowing the employment of one apprentice for a certain number of journeymen (the apprentice/journeyman ratio varying by trade), the ratio would become mandatory.

Shortly thereafter, the UCWA, dissatisfied with its lack of formal standing in the court decision, as well as the lack of progress made by minorities subsequent to victory in court, renewed demonstrations in June 1972. On June 7, Judge Lindberg ordered that the apprentice/journeyman ratios be altered in accordance with the COAC recommendation.

The COAC was also again admonished to monitor the defendants' compliance more closely. To assist in this effort, the COAC was instructed to act through those agents it deemed necessary, presumably including the UCWA. The UCWA, however, found this unsatisfactory, as they had not been specifically named as the agent the COAC should employ. After another series of demonstrations, the court "clarified" its earlier order and stated that all apprenticeship applicants were to be referred first to the UCWA for screening and that the UCWA representatives were to sit on the COAC. At this time the judge also ordered that the Department of Justice assign someone in the Seattle U.S. attorney's office full time to monitor the case.[9]

These events have brought some movement toward desegregation of the defendant unions. The alteration of the apprentice/journeyman ratio has been

TABLE 2.9

Apprentices, Graduates, and Goals by Craft, Seattle, December 1975

	Ironworkers	Plumbers and Pipefitters	Sheet Metal Workers	Electricians
First-year apprentices	19	18	11	15
Senior apprentices*	12	36	31	58
Graduates	28	28	19	8
Total	59	82	61	81
Goal	78	96	81	75
Percent of goal represented by senior apprentices and graduates	51.3	66.5	60.5	85.3

*Senior apprentices are defined as those beyond their first year of indenture.
Source: Quarterly Report to Judge Lindberg, December 1975.

particularly effective in opening new training opportunities and has additionally made the normal union grievance procedures available to aggrieved minorities.

However, the crafts are still generally short of the goals set for them by the court. Table 2.9 gives the number of apprentices and graduates for each local as of December 1975. Allowing for normal attrition rates among apprentices, none of the crafts is in compliance, although some progress had been made in the five and one-half years since the original order.

What factors have been important in determining the level of effectiveness of this decision? As mentioned above, progress has generally been conditioned on the balance of power between the UCWA and the unions. The ability of the UCWA to maintain the constant threat of renewed demonstrations over an extended period of time has been one of the most important factors in keeping the decision at least partially enforced.

It is extremely doubtful that the progress toward desegregation which has been made would have occurred as quickly without the activism of the UCWA. The UCWA has, by prodding the courts to enforce the law, forced the unions to accept more blacks than they otherwise would have. The role of the UCWA in providing qualified black applicants to the unions has also made it impossible for the unions to argue further that segregation is merely a matter of standards.

The COAC has proved to be a useful tool for insulating Judge Lindberg from the day-to-day acrimony between the parties. Further, some socialization has obviously taken place on the committee over the period since the original decision. The recent meetings have seen a much more cooperative spirit than earlier meetings.

For example, in 1974 the parties agreed, without direct judicial interference, to do away with special apprenticeship programs and to concentrate entirely on the regular programs. It was found that the special apprentices were not well trained enough to perform the required work of the craft. Most of the remaining special apprentices transferred to the regular program voluntarily.

Although the UCWA continued to argue that the program's failure was more a result of the unions' unwillingness to change their apprenticeship programs than a result of any conceptual weakness in the notion of accelerating apprenticeship training, they nevertheless agreed to the revision. Such an agreement would have been unthinkable as late as 1972.

The credit for this spirit of semidetente, it is generally recognized, goes to Professor Rieke, who appears to have convinced both sides to adopt a modified spirit of compromise. The agreement was incorporated into a consent decree made on March 12, 1974, which abolished the special apprenticeship programs and for the first time established a set of goals linked to a definite timetable by which compliance could be measured.

Judge Lindberg himself has, of course, played an important role in enforcement of the decree and probably would have been an important force even without the prodding of the UCWA. His behavior has been unique in Title

VII litigation in the construction industry both because of the specificity of the original order and because of the large number of supplemental decrees.

The judge has stated that he views this case as one of the two most important decisions of his career. Consequently, since the original decree, he has devoted a great deal of his resources both in and out of the courtroom to refinement of the principles involved.

Moreover, since the judge went into semiretirement and cut his work load shortly after the Ironworkers Local 86 decision, he had relatively more time to spend with the case. Many potential conflicts have been resolved without a formal decree by the judge's engaging in moral suasion through the COAC.

The Lindberg decision, as it is called, is at the minimum an example of how an activist judge in conjunction with an activist aggrieved party (the UCWA) can force the construction trades closer to equal employment opportunity. At best it may provide a prescription for that goal.

For proof of the relative effectiveness of this order, we need look no farther than the Seattle building trade unions which are not covered by the order but rather fall under the Seattle-King County hometown plan. Although reliable figures on minority representation in the other crafts are not available, it is generally conceded that although they were subject to basically the same outside stimuli as the crafts under the court order, they lag behind the crafts which are under the court order.

U.S. V. LATHERS LOCAL 46
(NEW YORK)

Local 46 of the Wood, Wire, and Metal Lathers International Union has jurisdiction in New York City and three counties of southern New York state (Nassau, Suffolk, and Westchester). The local retains control not only over metallic lathing and furring ("inside" work) but also over concrete reinforcement ("outside" work). Inside work can be done only by union members, but outside work—normally performed by ironworkers—can be done by either union members or permit men.

Permit men are not considered union members and undergo no apprenticeship program but are allowed to work during peak demand periods. Between 1968 and 1970, the membership of Local 46 (including journeymen and apprentices) varied between 1,450 and 1,500. In 1970 there were approximately 2,000 permit workers.

In 1967 a black journeyman lather from Florida was denied the opportunity to transfer into Local 46. At the request of the NAACP, the Department of Justice initiated an investigation of Local 46's employment practices. The investigation substantiated the complaint and discovered further evidence of discrimination.

As a result, the U.S. attorney for the southern district of New York filed a Title VII suit in May 1968 against Lathers Local 46 and its Joint Apprenticeship Training Committee (JATC). The government's complaint alleged that there existed a pattern and practice of resistance to nonwhite employment. The government charged that:

Lathers Local 46 was engaged in patterns and practices the purpose and effect of which were to exclude blacks from the union and to replace nonunion black lathers with white members and other white persons. The government noted that only four of the union's approximately 1,450 members were non-white and that although members and other whites were routinely issued permits, no blacks were issued permits until 1966. At the time of the suit, there were approximately 45 black permit holders.

Lathers Local 46 had adopted and was implementing a policy which prevented the transfer of black journeyman lathers into the union.

Lathers Local 46 was affording job referral opportunities to members and other whites not provided to blacks with equivalent qualifications. A rule requiring any individual seeking lathing work to "shape" the hiring hall (that is, to report in person to the hiring hall on a regular basis to attest to one's availability for work and to personally receive dispatches to available jobs) was not enforced in the case of the nearly all-white union membership. Further, permit holders were sometimes referred on the basis of race and nepotism rather than on the ability to perform the required work.

The JATC was discriminating on the basis of race in admissions to the apprenticeship program.

Both Lathers Local 46 and its JATC had failed to eliminate the effects of past discriminatory behavior.[10]

After a year and a half of pleading and motions, and on the eve of the trial (February 1970), the parties entered into a consent decree. Generally, the agreement enjoined Local 46 and the JATC from further discriminatory behavior. There were, however, several important specific elements in the decree.

First, the decree called for a restructuring of the local's referral practices. Only experience in the trade could be used as a basis for preference and then only if it related to the ability of workers to perform the required work. The union was to present detailed rules and procedures to implement these provisions within six months of the time the agreement became effective.

Second, the union was required to file monthly reports on the racial composition of its membership and permit holders and on the regular hours and overtime worked by each category of workers.

Third, the agreement called for the appointment of an administrator who would mediate disputes between the parties and implement the necessary administrative machinery. The administrator was also to seek agreement between the parties on a set of rules which would implement the equal employment opportunities guaranteed elsewhere in the agreement. With the concurrence of both parties, George Moskowitz, a veteran labor attorney and arbitrator, was named the administrator.

Nine months after the consent decree was signed (November 1970), the U.S. attorney, dissatisfied with progress toward implementation of the agreement, asked that Local 46 and the JATC be found in contempt of court. The government charged that the parties had failed, within the required six-month period, to begin significantly to correct their discriminatory practices.

It was alleged that the union had failed to inform those working under its jurisdiction of the new rules for the operation of the hiring hall and that in fact the rule requiring those seeking work to "shape" the hall was strictly enforced only in the case of nonwhites. The government further contended that the union was continuing its practice of discrimination in work and overtime assignments. The statistics reported in Table 2.10 were offered as evidence. It was argued that the earnings differentials were more than could be accounted for by experience differences. In May 1971 the court found Lathers Local 46 and the JATC in contempt.

The most important actions of the court at this time were to strengthen the role of the administrator and to award back pay to those individuals who had been discriminated against since the original order. The administrator was allowed to implement a computerized records system to keep track of union membership and permits issued and of the number of hours worked in each category.

Moskowitz also required that the JATC immediately inaugurate a nonwhite class of 25 members and that the local give out 250 permits per year, 125

TABLE 2.10

Employment and Pay Statistics for Local 46, New York, March–July 1970

Classification	Average Earnings for Those Who Worked (dollars)
Local 46	
White	3,855
Nonwhite	3,016
Permit Holders	
White	2,210
Nonwhite	1,989

Source: Government Posttrial Brief, 68 Civ. 2116.

TABLE 2.11

Construction Volume in Jurisdiction of Local 46,
New York, 1967–73
(thousands of dollars)

Year	Amount
1967	1,480,457
1968	1,829,186
1969	1,692,587
1970	1,854,470
1971	2,133,067
1972	2,356,098
1973	2,002,350

Source: New York Division of Housing and Community Renewals (based on building permits issued, also includes Rockland County).

of which must be given to nonwhites. Two New York City outreach organizations, the Recruitment and Training Program and Harlem Fight Back, were given the primary responsibility for providing qualified applicants. These events caused considerable resentment on the part of the union membership, which in turn stiffened the resistance of union officials toward integration.

As of July 1974, two groups of 125 nonwhites had been given permits. About 20 percent of the union's permit holders were thus nonwhite (the New York SMSA is 23.4 percent nonwhite). The class of 25 nonwhite apprentices admitted in 1971 (all of whom remain in the local) was the last apprenticeship class begun. The union membership (including apprentices) is thus about 2 percent nonwhite.

The record system indicates, however—for both union members and permit holders—that whites and nonwhites of the same skill level are now working approximately the same number of hours. This is true despite an overall decline in the number of hours worked due to a drop in construction activity during 1973 (see Table 2.11).

What has the overall impact of the lathers case been on equal employment opportunity in the New York City building trades? The suit must be assessed in relation to the total effort to desegregate the building trades beginning in the early 1960s. The situation in 1962 has been described as follows:

[In 1962] . . . there were no black journeymen or apprentices in the elevator constructors, ironworkers, metal lathers, sheet metal workers and steamfitters trades in the New York City building and construction industry. There were a few in the electricians, operating engineers, and plumbers. This pattern prevailed throughout the country.

Black workers are well represented in the so-called trowel-trades of the building and construction industry. They have constituted roughly 26 percent of construction laborers, 27 percent of the cement and concrete finishers, 16 percent of the plasterers, and about 12 percent of the nation's bricklayers. The pay is good—anywhere from $4.00 to $5.00 an hour for these are union jobs and require a high order of skills. But the work is dependent upon the weather and lacks status for it is uncertain, dirty and hard. Moreover, since the building industry is organized by crafts, there is virtually no way for a laborer, say, to work his way into the cleaner, better paid and steadier mechanical crafts—electricians, plumbers, steamfitters, ironworkers and sheet metal workers. Within these apprenticeable skilled trades, fathers passed their jobs on to their sons or nephews, excluding almost all outsiders. Roughly 4.5 percent of all the new workers entering these five crafts over the decade 1950 to 1960 were black. Yet, the percentage of all the workers within those crafts who are black changed only slightly, rising from 1.9 percent to 2.4 percent in ten years.[11]

Aside from the lathers case, desegregation pressure on the building trades has come primarily from three areas.

Outreach Programs

Frustration in the black community over the poor representation of blacks in construction jobs, particularly when the jobs were in black neighborhoods, surfaced in 1963 in the form of numerous construction-site shutdowns. This resulted in the establishment of a number of minority-based outreach organizations which searched the minority community for both qualified apprenticeship applicants and skilled individuals who might qualify for advance journeyman placement.

Most of these New York agencies have been short-lived and have enjoyed only meager success. The most successful has been the Recruitment and Training Program, founded by the Workers Defense League in 1963 and currently funded by the Department of Labor. RTP has been able to maintain credibility in the minority communities and at the same time enlist the suprt of the powerful leaders of the New York Building Trades Council (for example, the ex-secretary of the council, Peter Brennan, formerly U.S. secretary of labor). RTP has used this leverage in New York City over the past ten years to enroll over 2,500 youths in apprenticeship programs and to place over 800 individuals as journeymen or trainees.

Contract Compliance Efforts

The City of New York has been extremely active in the area of contract compliance. In conjunction with state and federal efforts, the net result has been a high level of pressure for minority employment, at least on government jobs. It is illustrative that in July 1974, New York City sued the Department of Labor over the department's approval of a hometown plan with minority bid specifications lower than the New York City ordinance. The case was decided in December 1974 for New York City.

Other Title VII Litigation

Three other Title VII lawsuits in addition to the lathers case have been filed by the Department of Justice against New York City labor unions (*U.S. v. Steamfitters Local 638, U.S. v. Sheet Metal Workers Local 28*, and *U.S. v. Operating Engineers Local 15*). Although limitations on space preclude an individual discussion of these cases here, the successfully prosecuted cases—the steamfitters and the sheet metal workers (the operating engineers case is not yet settled)—must be considered to have an impact on building trades employment at least equal to the lathers case (and perhaps greater, since each of these unions has a larger membership).

The above efforts have brought about some gains in minority employment in the New York City construction trades. Table 2.12 reports the number of minority journeymen for both the general and the mechanical trades in the early

TABLE 2.12

Minority Representation in New York City Construction Trades (years individual unions were surveyed vary from 1969 to 1973)

Trade	Total Journeymen	Minority Journeymen	Percent Minorities
General construction trades	54,194	11,086	20.5
Laborers only	5,800	1,425	24.6
Mechanical trades*	24,990	1,387	5.6
Total	79,184	12,473	15.8

*Mechanical trades include boilermakers, electricians, elevator constructors, ironworkers, plumbers, steamfitters, and sheet metal workers.
Source: New York City Office of Contract Compliance.

1970s. Even considering that these data do not include recent minority gains in apprenticeship programs, it can be seen that further efforts toward equal employment opportunity are necessary, especially in the mechanical trades. This is particularly clear when the figures in Table 2.12 are considered relative to the fact that the population of New York City is 23.4 percent nonwhite.

In summary, the Local 46 case has been but one of a number of important and complex factors which have initiated the modest gains which have been made with respect to minority employment in the New York City building trades.

The demonstrable impact of the suit can be seen in the meager gains inside Local 46 itself. However, there was clearly a demonstration effect on other unions who saw that the government is willing to file contempt charges when unions ignore court orders and that judges are willing to award back pay when it is deemed necessary. But the impact of such an effect of the case is difficult to assess accurately.

CONCLUSIONS

The evidence from the five examples of Title VII litigation in the construction industry indicates that enforcement of Title VII (or some close substitute such as contractor compliance) is a necessary but insufficient condition for promoting equal employment opportunity in the building trades.

Moreover, the evidence indicates that legal sanctions have been invoked only after pressure for them has arisen from an aggrieved minority organization. It seems unlikely that any of the progress which has been made toward desegregation in the above cases would have occurred because of voluntary action alone. Civil rights activism and consequent legal sanctions are necessary to get the attention of those who would discriminate in the construction industry.

From the time a violation is discovered, however, we must be careful not to overrate the positive impact of legal proceedings. The error could be made of assuming that all progress toward desegregation of the construction industry since the passage of the 1964 Civil Rights Act is due to Title VII. Other factors may have intervened independently.

Legal proceedings are a slow, resource-consuming process. Table 2.13 indicates the severity of this problem. The table reports the time elapsed from the filing of the original complaint to various stages in the legal process. For example, the average time between the initial complaint and the district court decision (or in the case of *U.S. v. Lathers Local 46*, the consent decree) was at least one year and four months. Table 2.13 also provides some rough estimates of the resource costs of this type of litigation. *U.S. v. Ironworkers Local 86* alone required almost 6,000 lawyer hours.

TABLE 2.13

Time and Resource Costs of Litigation

Case	Title VII Complaint Filed	First Decision (time elapsed)	Appellate Decision (time elapsed)	Type of Latest Supplemental Action	Estimated Department of Justice Lawyer Years	Other Department of Justice Costs	Estimated Union Lawyer Years	Other Union Costs
U.S. v. Sheet Metal Workers Local 36 St. Louis	2-66	3-68 (2 yrs., 1 mo.)	9-69 (3 yrs., 7 mos.)	None			3/4	
Local 53 v. Vogler New Orleans	12-66	1-68 (1 yr., 1 mo.)	1-69 (2 yrs., 1 mo.)	None				
Dobbins v. Local 212 Cincinnati	7-67	9-68 (1 yr., 2 mos.)	None	Court order 10-68				
U.S. v. Lathers 46 New York	5-68	2-70 (1 yr., 9 mos.)	None	Refusal to stay contempt order 3-72	3	Research analysts	2½	$135,000 back pay and maintenance of computer system
U.S. v. Local 86 Seattle	11-69	6-70 (7 mos.)	2-71 (1 yr., 3 mos.)	Consent order 3-75	4	Research analysts per diem for lawyers in Seattle	3	

Source: Interviews with Department of Justice and union attorneys. All the estimates were approximate as Department of Justice does not keep time logs and union attorneys would not reveal time logs. All individuals were asked to include time spent on related proceedings.

Each of the cases discussed above is unique, and many of the principles established in a particular case may not be of general applicability. It is consequently difficult to avoid fighting segregation on a case-by-case basis. Such a strategy is very expensive.

In addition, civil rights law is better suited to combating overt discrimination than changing the institutionalized patterns which permeate the construction industry. While attacking overt discrimination may eventually change institutionalized patterns, legal sanctions have the potential for causing a hardening of racial barriers and therefore actually slowing change, as the Lathers Local 46 case in New York City well illustrates.

In order to increase minority participation in the construction industry, we recommend that the Department of Labor take the following steps:

Strengthen the outreach concept and make it applicable to journeymen as well as apprentices. We have very little evidence that many qualified minority journeymen are being denied access to construction employment, but there is no better way to discover this than through outreach programs. In our judgment, the outreach concept was one of the most effective developments arising from the efforts to get blacks into the construction industry during the 1960s; outreach programs were conspicuous in producing results where other activities failed.

Minority workers who almost meet union journeyman standards could be upgraded through special training programs. A program might be adopted to identify minority contractors who—with a little training and technical assistance—could meet industry standards. Although it would be unwise to expect a significant impact on construction labor supplies from upgrading the few existing minority contractors, these contractors are organized and could provide skilled craftsmen.[12]

Attention should be given to developing written objective procedures to determine minimum standards for journeyman status in the building trades. We have no evidence that current standards and procedures are unreasonable, but tripartite review panels (comprised of representatives of employers, unions, and the general public) might be established to review specific standards and to provide appeals procedures for minorities who feel unfairly treated by local unions or employers. It is difficult to resolve the question of whether there are many qualified minority journeymen unless objective standards are established and subject to review.

Rather than the hometown and imposed plans, which rarely seem to be very effective, national agreements should be worked out to provide industry-wide mechanisms for recruiting, training, and placing minorities in the construction industry. Plans which attach workers to jobs rather than to the labor market are not likely to be very effective, because the concept of a specific job is much less meaningful in the construction industry than in an industrial plant.

• Although there are problems of representation by the parties at the national level, these problems are nowhere near as intense as in local agreements. Moreover, local agreements rarely coincide with labor markets and usually relate only to federal or unionized construction industries. National agreements could specify the mechanisms for admitting minorities, while specific agreements could be worked out at the local level.

• National agreements would also add the moral authority of national labor and employer associations and would relieve some of the political pressures on local union officials, who are most vulnerable to attack for racial reasons.

• The guidelines for national agreements might include that agreements should be adopted for unionized and nonunion branches of the industry; outreach programs should be adopted to recruit and train minority apprentices and journeymen; and parties to the agreements should include representatives of minorities, workers, employers, and the Department of Labor (OFCC).

The matter of goals and timetables is a troublesome one and creates the feeling by whites that quotas are being required, despite protestations that goals do not equal quotas and merely require good-faith efforts. However, unions and contractors are understandably nervous about charges of preferential treatment for blacks and fear a weakening of standards.

It is our view that outreach programs will eventually make imposed goals and timetables unnecessary. We have noted that the goals assigned outreach programs usually are considered minimum targets, while those in the imposed and hometown plans are considered maximums.

NOTES

1. H. Hill, "Evading the Law," *Civil Rights Digest*, Summer 1974, p. 5.

2. The full legal citations for these cases are as follows: *United States v. Sheet Metal Workers International Association, Local Union No. 36, AFL-CIO*, 280 F. Supp. 719 (E.D. Mo. 1968), on appeal, 416 F.2d 123 (8th Cir. 1969); *Vogler v. McCarty, Inc., United States by Clark v. Local 53 of the International Association of Heat and Frost Insulators and Asbestos Workers*, 294 F. Supp. 368 (E.D. La. 1968), *Local 53 of the International Association of Heat and Frost Insulators and Asbestos Workers v. Vogler*, 407 F.2d 1047 (5th Cir. 1969); *Dobbins v. Local 212, International Brotherhood of Electrical Workers, AFL-CIO, United States v. International Brotherhood of Electrical Workers, Local 212*, 292 F. Supp. 413 (S.D. Ohio W.D. 1968); *United States v. Local 86, International Association of Bridge, Structural, Ornamental and Reinforcing Ironworkers*, 315 F. Supp. 1202 (W.D. Wash. 1970), 443 F.2d 433 (9th Cir. 1971); and *United States v. Wood, Wire, and Metal Lathers International Union, Local Union 46*, 328 F. Supp. 429 (S.D. N.Y. 1971), further order, 341 F. Supp. 694, on appeal, 471 F.2d 408.

3. St. Louis Supplemental Manpower Agreement, Article IV (Goals).

4. 294 F. Suppl 368 (E.D. La. 1968).

5. Ibid.

6. M. Liggett, *Employment Patterns of Blacks and Women in Cincinnati* (Washington, D.C.: Equal Employment Opportunity Commission, 1971), p. 12.

7. F. Ray Marshall and Vernon Briggs, *The Negro and Apprenticeship* (Baltimore: Johns Hopkins University Press, 1967).

8. 8616 W.D. Wash. (1970).

9. For another review of these events, see W. Gould, "The Seattle Building Trades Industry: The First Comprehensive Relief against Employment Discrimination in the Construction Industry," *Stanford Law Review*, April 1974, pp. 773–813.

10. 2116 S.D. N.Y. (1968).

11. T. Brooks, *Black Builders: A Job Program That Works* (New York: League for Industrial Democracy, 1970), pp. 3–4.

12. Robert W. Glover, *Minority Enterprise in Construction* (New York: Praeger, 1978).

3

COMBATING EMPLOYMENT DISCRIMINATION IN HIRING, UPGRADING, AND SENIORITY THROUGH CONTRACT COMPLIANCE: THE CASE OF SHIPBUILDING

Shipbuilding, with the exception of the experiments with the modular method of construction made popular in Japan, remains even in the twentieth century a labor-intensive, craft-oriented industry.[1] Work is geared to orders in both shipbuilding and ship repair, which means that the number of persons employed fluctuates with the volume of business. Some yards have sought to diversify their offerings so that they can provide steady work for their employees.[2] These efforts, however, have not changed the labor intensiveness of the industry.

The five cases in this study focus on coastal shipbuilding and repair (Standard Industrial Classification [SIC] code 373). Authority for assuring compliance with equal employment opportunity provisions under Executive Order 11246 rests with the Office of Civil Rights in the Maritime Administration of the Department of Commerce.

On-site interviews with personnel bring out two outstanding characteristics of the large shipyards. First, the yards conduct an impressive amount of training in shipbuilding crafts. A large shipyard is a training institution.

Second, every personnel official complains about the high rate of voluntary terminations. Hence, shipyards spend an enormous amount of their resources in training people, knowing that many of them will leave the industry. However frustrating this must be for the managements of the various yards, it should be noted that shipyards perform a social (training) role in this regard.

A major reason for the high exit rate, voluntary terminations, or turnover is the kind of working conditions that exist when ships are built. The job description for a ship's painter, drawn up by a major shipbuilder, includes in its working conditions extremes of cold and heat plus temperature changes, wet and humid conditions, noise and vibration, electrical, mechanical, and explosive hazards, and fumes and odors resulting from toxic conditions, dust, or poor ventilation.[3]

TABLE 3.1

U.S. Shipbuilding: Value of Contract Awards Including Major Ship Conversions, by Category of Funding, 1964-74

Fiscal Year	Total Value (millions of dollars)	Percentage Shares			
		Navy	Maritime Administration (subsidized)	Total Public Subsidized	Private Subsidized
1964	795.8	73.0	19.1	92.6	7.4
1965	1,048.5	75.6	16.1	91.7	8.3
1966	769.8	60.0	35.2	95.2	4.8
1967	681.8	72.1	5.4	77.5	22.5
1968	1,193.7	52.8	25.9	78.7	21.3
1969	652.9	25.1	40.3	65.4	34.6
1970	1,206.8	73.4	9.0	82.4	17.6
1971	1,213.3	63.8	29.1	92.9	7.1
1972	2,286.9	52.0	34.8	86.8	13.2
1973	1,733.1	21.4	72.7	94.1	5.9
1974	3,986.0	53.0	19.0	72.0	28.1
Total, 1964-74 ($)	15,568.6	8,454.4	4,476.4	12,930.8	2,637.8
Percent	100.0	54.3	28.8	83.1	16.9

Note: Percentages may not add to 100.0 because of rounding.
Source: Maritime Administration.

Finally, U.S. shipbuilding is clearly dependent on the federal government, particularly the Department of Defense, for new hardware and repair orders and on the Maritime Administration for subsidies for the construction of commercial ships.

The heavy reliance of shipyards on government support is reflected in industry statistics. As shown in Table 3.1, 83.1 percent of the industry's contracts for new ships or major ship conversions over the 11-year period between July 1, 1964, and June 30, 1975, can be attributed to public funding. Naval contracts alone accounted for more than a majority of the work. The Maritime Administration reported that as of January 1, 1975, there were 63 naval vessels under construction or on order.

The five cases chosen for this study fall into a growth and decline pattern. Three of the yards have been growth yards in most of the years under study, although one of them had to recover from a sharp loss in business associated with sanctions imposed on it by the Department of Commerce. The two West Coast yards have experienced sharp declines in the number of employees.

This contrast allows us to put into sharp relief the impact the growth in employment has had on EEO compliance. Our growth yards include the Alabama Dry Dock and Shipbuilding Company, the Newport News Shipbuilding and Dry Dock Company, and the Ingalls Shipbuilding Division of Litton Industries. The two yards that experienced a sharp loss of orders are the Lockheed and Todd yards in Seattle.

THE OFFICE OF CIVIL RIGHTS IN THE MARITIME ADMINISTRATION

The Maritime Administration has its headquarters in Washington, D.C., with regional offices in New York, New Orleans, and San Francisco. There are subregional offices in Seattle and Long Beach. (For a time the New York regional Office of Civil Rights stationed an employee in Norfolk to monitor the Newport News yard, but that office was closed in 1971.) The total staff of the Office of Civil Rights (OCR) comprises some 40 persons (see Figure 1).

Under Order 4 issued to implement Executive Order 11246, government contractors were required to prepare detailed affirmative action plans containing goals and timetables. When Executive Order 11246 was amended by Executive Order 11375 (which added consideration of females to prohibitions based on race, color, and national origin), Order 4 was revised to include sex also. Hence the operative authority for implementation has been Order 4 and Revised Order 4.

The work of the OCR is conducted through the medium of two basic documents: affirmative action plans and compliance review reports. Affirmative action plans show job-holding patterns in great detail, with separate reporting by sex and four minority groups: blacks, Spanish-surnamed Americans, Orientals or American Asians, and American Indians. The affirmative action plans contain goals and timetables for each sex and each minority group annually. These plans are filed yearly, but occasionally the OCR negotiates changes in the annual plans.

The compliance review reports are conducted periodically. The rules for periodic reviews are somewhat flexible, part of that flexibility reflecting the low staffing levels of the office. In general, an attempt is made to review each of the 30 large yards—which have about 80 percent of the total employment of the industry—every six months. The smaller yards (about 60 in number) are scheduled for annual reviews, but not all of these take place. When a yard, large or small, gets its "house in order," the frequency of compliance reviews is reduced.

Compliance reviews are conducted by two different methods: a desk audit and an on-site review. Desk audits and on-site reviews are preceded by consider-

FIGURE 1

Organizational Structure of Office of Civil Rights, Maritime Administration

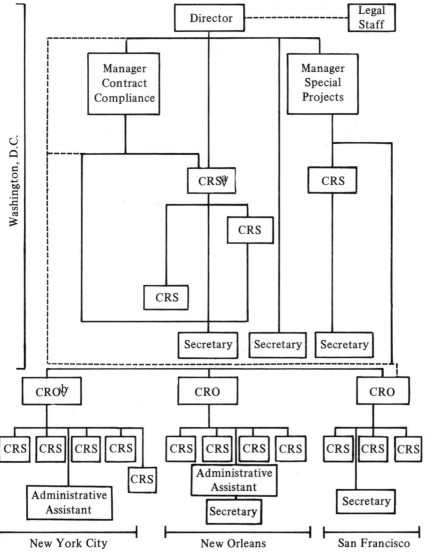

ᵃCRS = Civil Rights Specialist, since renamed Equal Opportunity Specialist (EOS).
ᵇCRO = Civil Rights Officer.

———— Direct lines of communication and authority.

‐ ‐ ‐ ‐ ‐ Lines of technical assistance and direction.

Source: Lester Rubin, *Measures of Effectiveness of the Office of Civil Rights, U.S. Maritime Administration* (Philadelphia: University of Pennsylvania, 1973), p. 41.

able amounts of statistical material filed by the contractors and reviewed by the compliance officer, who works under the title of equal opportunity specialist. The regional staff members do the desk audits and on-site reviews, but their work must be approved by the senior compliance officer in the Washington, D.C., headquarters.

Briefly, the compliance procedure reviews and approves the affirmative action plan, and ensures through the continuing surveillance of audits and reviews that the approved affirmative action plans are implemented.* The compliance effort of the OCR is an example of a continuous relationship rather than an episodic one (such as that between the EEOC and respondents).

This study is concerned with the period since 1968, when the OCR was established in the Maritime Administration. Interest centers on the use of out-of-court settlements as a means of achieving compliance with Executive Order 11246 as amended.

This procedure has also been examined by Rubin, but with the use of an entirely different technique.[4] A perspective on the historical role played by blacks in shipbuilding has also been provided by Rubin.[5]

THE NEWPORT NEWS STORY

The Newport News Shipbuilding and Dry Dock Company dates back to 1886, when it was built by the Huntington family. Family control lasted until 1927, when it was replaced by a New York-based investor group. In 1968 the yard was absorbed by a conglomerate, Tenneco, Inc.

Blacks have always been employed in the yard, but the pattern of job holding did not quite fit the traditional Southern black/white job dichotomy. Segregation by job assignment was a fact of life in the yard until very recently, but it did not mean that blacks could not achieve first-class mechanic status. Blacks achieved this status most commonly in the less-desirable departments. With few exceptions (and these late in the history of the yard), supervisory jobs were restricted to whites.

From the beginning, the Huntington family made a commitment to hire blacks commensurate with their percentage in the labor force in the Newport

---

*There is another compliance tool available to the OFCC and other agencies: the Pre-award clearance review. The contractor cannot receive a government contract unless the supervising agency gives a preaward clearance, indicating that the contractor is "in compliance." This clearance is usually given on the basis of having an approved affirmative action plan in operation. Hence, the ruling determination with respect to being "contract awardable" is made when an affirmative action plan is accepted. The preaward clearance has rarely been used by the OCR.

News area. The family was so concerned about this tradition that the contract of sale in 1927 carried with it the unusual provision that the new owners maintain a level of black employment similar to or above that of black participation in the local labor market. Further, even though much influenced by the pattern of race relations in in southern Virginia, the yard continued to produce black first-class mechanics.

At least two observers of the yard noticed the effect of this kind of place-ment. Northrup, in his 1944 review of the impact of unions on black employ-ment opportunities, observed that

> the Newport News Company has employed large numbers of Negroes since it commenced operations in 1886. In November 1942, its 8,200 Negro employees comprised 27.4 percent of its total working force. Although Negroes are employed in many skilled capacities, they are, for the most part, denied employment as elec-tricians, machinists, and welders. Moreover, Negroes are not admitted to the company's apprentice training school.[6]

Following the highly touted conciliation agreement at the yard by the combined forces of the federal government in 1966, Blumrosen, a member of the EEOC, noted:

> In 1965 there were at least 400 Negro employees who were in the top group of job classifications called mechanic. This meant that there was a reservoir of trained skilled manpower from which super-visory employees could be identified. In most Southern plants three years ago it would have been impossible to find a substantial number of Negroes who had been promoted to first-class mechanic status.[7]

The pride of the Newport News yard is its apprentice school. This company-run vocational education school combines academic and on-the-job training for would-be shipbuilders for a four-year schooling program. Students who wish to become designers continue in training for a fifth year.

Consistent with the patterns of exclusion found throughout U.S. industry in the past, blacks were simply not allowed entry into the apprentice school. The color bar was not broken until 1956. Since that time things have changed but largely under threat of federal government interference. In December 1973, 14.4 percent of the apprentices then enrolled were black.

A similar pattern of exclusion existed in the clerical occupations outside the production and maintenance operations. The first black clerical worker, a secretary, was hired in 1956. In January 1974, 32.7 percent of the office workers at the yard were black.

The Actors and the Environment:
A Southern Setting

The Newport News story is really a two-act play. Some new actors appear in the second act, others drop out, and still others have their roles modified. The first conciliation agreement was concluded on March 30, 1966; the second was consummated on June 12, 1970.

The corporate managers and some of the personnel officials at the time of the 1966 conciliation agreement were replaced by Tenneco functionaries before the bargaining that led to the June 1970 settlement. The union is the independent Peninsula Shipbuilders Association, which grew out of the old Bethlehem plan. The union officials remained the same, but between the two acts, two of them were incarcerated in the county jail for defying a court order during the only strike in the history of the yard.

In the 1966 case, the government team was led by the EEOC, with the assistance of representatives of the Departments of Justice, Defense, and Labor. In the second case, the government team was led by the OCR, with assistance from the Department of Labor.

The local NAACP, whose president was an employee of the yard and a charging party in an early EEOC case, was involved in the first case and received assistance from the NAACP Legal Defense Fund. There was no formal organized resistance to government efforts among white workers at the yard. In addition, surprisingly, for a case of this size, there was only a small amount of outside legal assistance.

Newport News lies at the end of a peninsula that is bordered on one side by the James River and on the other by the Hampton Roads portion of the Chesapeake Bay. The shipyard has long been the dominant employer and influence in the town. The leadership in the yard, from the Huntington family through the investor group that held the facility through 1968, considered Newport News to be "its town." Put another way, no one ever needed to be reminded that "what is good for the Newport News Dry Dock and Shipbuilding Company is good for Newport News." The present Tenneco management team represents a break from the paternalistic patterns of the past.

Until quite recently, race relations have been rigidly segregationist in the town and at the yard—so much so that when restroom facilities were integrated at the yard prior to a launching ceremony featuring President Dwight D. Eisenhower as the honored guest, Virginia law was violated. It was only in the mid-1960s that this part of Virginia began to comply with the 1954 Supreme Court decision concerning school segregation.

Newport News—a small southern town with a tradition of well-defined racial roles—has a strong streak of religiosity (of the Protestant, largely Baptist kind) running through its daily existence. Although there has been a heavy concentration of federal military bases (primarily navy) since World War I and especially since World War II, the traditionally conservative view of the world springing from the James River peninsula has been altered little.

Unemployment rates for the Newport News-Hampton area are shown in Tables 3.2 and 3.3. These calculations are made on a place-of-residence basis, and the area covered was expanded beginning in 1970. For most of the years studied in this case, the unemployment rate was below 3 percent. In addition, the local unemployment rate was below the national rate in every year.

The volume of employment at the shipyard increased every year from 1966 except for the change from 1973 to 1974. Hence, the yard was drawing new employees from a tight labor market throughout the entire period. Further, the yard was offering work to potential shipbuilders, who traditionally show high termination rates.

The OCR and the personnel officials at the yard have agreed that the appropriate labor market for the facility is the SMSA embracing Newport News-Hampton and York County. In 1960 the black population of this SMSA was about 28 percent; the 1970 census indicates that this percentage dropped to about 26 percent.

The Blumrosen Agreement

The EEOC began to function on July 2, 1965. On March 30, 1966, the commission, with the assistance of the Departments of Defense, Labor, and Justice, concluded a major conciliation agreement with the Newport News Shipbuilding and Dry Dock Company that has been the subject of some controversy; at times, this controversy has deteriorated into acrimony.[8]

TABLE 3.2

Rate of Unemployment by Year, Newport News-Hampton Area, 1965-69

Year	Unemployment Rate (percent)
1965	2.6
1966	2.5
1967	2.7
1968	2.6
1969	2.8

Source: Revised Labor Force Components, Newport News-Hampton Area, 1965-69, supplied by Virginia Employment Commission.

TABLE 3.3

Rate of Unemployment by Year, Newport News–Hampton Metropolitan Area, 1970–73

Year	Unemployment Rate (percent)
1970	4.0
1971	3.2
1972	2.8
1973	2.8

Source: Labor Market Trends for the years indicated. Published by the Virginia Employment Commission.

The settlement has been recorded as a conciliation agreement, but it was extracted through the use of the OFCC's power to withhold funds. Hence its official title of "conciliation agreement," used throughout this chapter, is somewhat of a euphemism.

A 1970 review of the conciliation agreement suggested that it was being reconsidered by the OCR, which proved to be an accurate observation.[9] What has come to be known as the Blumrosen agreement, after the then-chief negotiator for the EEOC, raises so many questions about the federal government's compliance efforts that it should be reviewed from our vantage point eight years later.

At least three facts combined to give the Blumrosen agreement landmark status. First, it was the first instance in which the combined forces of the EEOC and the Departments of Justice, Defense, and Labor were brought together in a civil rights case affecting employment. Second, the yard was the first major government contractor charged under Title VII of the Civil Rights Act of 1964. Third, the case attacked the personnel system at the yard in addition to encompassing a number of individual cases which had been brought against the facility. This combination made the case a very important one and certainly provided a boost to employee morale at the fledgling EEOC.

Several things were accomplished quickly and easily in the Newport News case. Segregated facilities were eliminated. The yard agreed to recruit blacks actively for jobs at all levels. The apprentice school was attacked on several points and made some important changes in procedures.

The selection committee, all white, was integrated by adding a black supervisor from the paint department. The age limits for entry were changed from 18 to 20 years to 18 to 25 years. The rule against marriage, either at entry or during the program, was dropped. The use of College Board scores as a screening device for entry was eliminated.

The selection board was ordered to notify all yard employees in the appropriate age category that applications would be accepted from them. In order to facilitate this, the yard also dropped its rule against accepting applicants who had previous college training. In addition, the yard agreed to actively recruit young blacks from area high schools for entrance into the apprentice school.

An additional problem was the selection of students for training courses other than those provided by the apprentice school. The yard is a training institution, and some charged that blacks were denied entrance into certain courses. This was rectified by specifying that blacks would be placed on an eligibility roster for the next open slot. This was the first instance found in this study of the use of the doctrine of "rightful place."

The rest of the agreement was more complex and generated considerable controversy. The EEOC charges against the yard required extensive examination of personnel records, which was acknowledged to require time and expertise. Hence the agreement called for an outside expert to be hired by the yard, at the agreement of both parties, who would do the statistical work.

The EEOC charges specified three points: the wages of black employees doing the same work as whites were lower than those of the white employees; black employees were promoted at a slower rate than white employees; and black employees were not promoted to supervisory status under the same circumstances as white employees.[10]

The outside expert selected was a management consulting group, Case and Company, which began work on the three issues listed above. There was not much substance to the charge that blacks were performing the same work as whites without receiving equal pay—with some thorny exceptions. No cases were found where blacks and whites were performing under the same job title and receiving different wages. This would, of course, have been a violation of the collective bargaining agreement as well as of Title VII.

Since no such cases were found, the analysis moved to the issue of classification procedures, which produced the same effect. This is a highly technical issue, as the court cases filed under the Equal Pay Act will attest, and much of the detail will be omitted. A single example should suffice, however: maids and porters often have similar duties, but the two titles receive different wages. The practices at Newport News were more complicated than this example, but Case and Company did find a few. The company agreed to reclassify the jobs, resulting in higher positions and concomitantly higher pay. However, no back pay was awarded, in this instance or at any other place in the agreement.

A difficult issue to resolve was that of the accuracy and magnitude of the charge that blacks were promoted at a slower rate than whites. Although it did not involve supervisory positions, this issue included all of the classifications falling below that of the first-line supervisor. Company officials to this day argue that the charge was unproven. Case and Company officials will not talk with outsiders.

The EEOC claimed that this portion of the agreement resulted in 3,980 promotions for blacks. The Peninsula Shipbuilders Association (the union) argues that the number was 155. A 1970 summary of the case identified more than 155 promotions, but although the exact number could not be determined, it was not close to 3,980.[11]

Promotions through the classes and from title to title occur very frequently at the yard. In some lines, an employee may move from one step to another in just a few months. Hence with roughly 5,000 black employees, it is not hard to imagine that there were 3,980 promotions for blacks in the year following the agreement. However, it is quite another point to attribute all of this movement to the agreement.

Promotions to first-line supervisor produced some real learning experiences for all students of fair employment practice enforcement. The agreement sought to correct past discrimination against blacks at the supervisory level. A profile of the last 100 white employees promoted to supervisor was compared with the qualifications of selected blacks. However, this method was abandoned, and Blumrosen's explanation was that the qualifications for supervisor were discovered to be so varied that the composite or profile was not a meaningful yardstick.

There can be no doubt regarding this finding. However, a competing explanation offered by some of the older personnel officials at the yard was that not one single black met the profile. However distressing, this should not have been a surprising discovery, since if an employer decides to ensure that no blacks will do supervisory work, it is highly likely that blacks will never gain the kinds of experience leading to supervisory responsibility. Hence, when a point-in-time study is called for, as in the case of the Blumrosen agreement, it will follow that blacks will lack the qualifications for supervisory positions. After all, it was company policy not to provide blacks that kind of experience.

In any event, a new program was worked out a year after the initial agreement. In the new approach, a profile was drawn by department of the last five whites promoted to supervisory status. Then blacks within each department were compared with the profile, ranked, and assigned a spot on a preferential list.

This has not worked well. Some 20 blacks were promoted before the new agreement was signed on March 31, 1967, a full year after the initial agreement. The preferential list for promotion to quarterman (a supervisory position) had about 70 names on it at that time. In March 1974, some 46 names still remained on the list.

One reason is that in small departments there has been very little turnover at the supervisory level. In addition, some have suggested that personnel officials have promoted other blacks around those on the list. In any event, this part of the agreement was, in effect, an object lesson in how *not* to negotiate a promotion plank in a discrimination case.

The original impetus for the case was a set of charges filed with the EEOC. By the time the parties reached agreement, charges had been filed by 41 persons. All of these charges were resolved within 90 days of the March 30, 1966, agreement.

It is difficult to make a brief assessment of the Blumrosen agreement. First, the art of bringing together so many government agencies acting in concert must be considered a first-rate achievement. Second, the agreement was an attempt to break a pattern of personnel operations that literally had its roots in the 1880s. The result, as Blumrosen himself said, "was to shatter the old system."

Certainly this "shattering of the old system" has to be the major achievement of the agreement, for it meant to the black community that "somebody out there cares." No amount of criticism of the details of the agreement can change the fact that blacks would see outsiders attempting to improve their employment conditions.

As mentioned earlier, several things were accomplished quickly and easily, and these will not be repeated here. The company was quick to apply the agreement, and no review by the EEOC has suggested that the yard has failed to live up to the agreement.

Several of the issues raised in the agreement continued to appear in charges filed by blacks with the EEOC and reported to compliance officials in the OCR. An on-site review in late 1969 indicated decisively that the yard would require extensive changes to effect compliance. In that sense, the Blumrosen agreement fell short of its goal.

Thus, the Newport News yard was destined to go through the wrenching process of hard bargaining with federal officials about its EEO stance a second time. This leads to a review of the June 12, 1970, agreement.

The June 12, 1970, Agreement

Employment discrimination did not disappear in the wake of the Blumrosen agreement. The big settlement—and the one that allowed, or perhaps compelled, the yard to turn the corner, came on June 12, 1970. Two organizational changes preceded this agreement.

In a 1968 reorganization of the OFCC efforts, the Department of Defense was relieved of its responsibility for EEO enforcement in the shipyards; this responsibility was transferred to the OCR (Department of Commerce). Also in 1968, Tenneco, Inc., a worldwide conglomerate, bought the Newport News Shipbuilding and Dry Dock Company.

In addition to the organizational changes affecting the yard, the OFCC issued Order 4, which calls for all government contractors under its jurisdiction to develop affirmative action plans with goals and timetables. These affirmative action plans have to be approved by the reviewing personnel of the responsible monitoring agency.

In late 1969 and early 1970, several events hastened an agreement. In late 1969 the staff of the eastern region of the OCR conducted a regular annual compliance review and after an intensive review of the records concluded that the yard was not in compliance.

Early in 1970 the OCR in Washington, D.C., under the leadership of a new director, Andrew Gibson, moved to correct the situation by delaying authorization to the company of funds for the laying of the keel for a nuclear aircraft carrier, the *Eisenhower* (a preaward denial of clearance).

Predictably, company top management appealed to congressional officials and the White House to overturn the decision. However, despite many trips to Capitol Hill and audiences with White House personnel, it became clear to the management at Newport News that the Maritime Administration would not yield.

A supplemental plan was worked out by the Maritime Administration and the yard, but just when these parties thought they had reached agreement, Art Fletcher, an assistant secretary in the Department of Labor, intervened and rejected the supplemental plan as inadequate. This led to further changes and strengthening of the supplemental affirmative action plan and eventual settlement in the form of the June 12, 1970, agreement.

The struggle had continued for five months, and it is clear that the Tenneco management desired to avoid another such confrontation. The new president of the Newport News yard issued a strong statement as the covering letter of the June 12, 1970, agreement.

In addition, the yard president brought in a special assistant—a black educator from the Newport News area—to work with the yard and the black community in the labor market. A special personnel officer with EEO responsibility was appointed to report directly to the vice-president in charge of personnel. This officer was assigned a black deputy (coincidentally, the first black to complete the apprentice school with training as a marine electrician).

Management made an effort to assure the black community that its EEO commitment was real, and this has proved to be the case.

An important part of the June 12 agreement was the special transfer program, which contained the concept of an affected class. The Blumrosen agreement had "groped for, but never quite developed adequately, the concept of [an] affected class."[12] No such problem arose with the June 12 agreement.

In the introduction to the section dealing with the special transfer program, the following explicit statement appeared:

> Prior to July 1, 1966, certain jobs within the Company were filled primarily by Negroes. Although many whites worked in those jobs and many Negroes worked in other jobs, there is at least a chance

that one of the factors leading to the placement and/or retention of Negroes in certain jobs was their color. As hereinafter indicated, a program will be undertaken to afford a new opportunity to such Negro employees.[13]

The agreement provided for rate retention ("red-circling") and transfer rights that would apply to members of the affected class. In addition, it spelled out goals and timetables for white-collar jobs and indicated the kinds of recruiting methods that the yard would use in applying the good-faith doctrine to its efforts at meeting goals and timetables.

The special transfer program was an effort to provide opportunities for employees who, because of their race, had been denied opportunities in the past. The agreement allowed 1,835 black employees to elect to move into other lines of progression. By January 1, 1974, 298—or roughly 16 percent—of the affected class had been transferred. Also as of that date, 28 applications for transfer remained on file.

The status of the 298 transfers as of January 1, 1974, is shown in Table 3.4. Ninety persons have completed the program; 144 are still in training. Even if all of these 234 persons could be assumed to have been successful in the program, that constitutes no more than 13 percent of those eligible. Although this specific program has produced meager results, blacks have done well in other areas of the yard, as shown in the following section.

TABLE 3.4

Special Transfer Program Status of Enrollees, Newport News, as of January 1, 1974

Current Status or Reason for Leaving Program	Number
Returned to original department of own volition	28
Returned to original department for medical reasons	7
Returned to original department for failure	19
Terminated	8
Deceased	2
Satisfied provisions of program	90
Presently in program	144
Total	298
Outstanding applications	28

Source: 1974 Affirmative Action Program for Equal Employment Opportunity at the Newport News Shipbuilding and Dry Dock Company, p. 58.

Perhaps one reason why more blacks did not elect to transfer was that transferees could not carry forward their yard seniority into the new line. The members of the class competed for openings among themselves on the basis of yard seniority, but those who moved both retained their seniority from the old line and accumulated separate seniority in the new line. As discussed subsequently, this kind of dual seniority was eventually rejected by the OCR at Alabama Dry Dock as being inadequate.

Overall Changes in Racial Employment Patterns

Black participation at the Newport News yard has never been a problem; the Huntington family decided that issue early, and no backsliding has occurred. Furthermore, blacks have been able to achieve first-class mechanic ratings for a long time. However, the segregation that existed in the community also was practiced at the yard.

The initial breaks in this pattern came during the decade of the 1950s, when the first black entered the apprentice school and the first black clerical was hired. The first concerted effort to break the segregated pattern of work conditions came with the Blumrosen agreement in 1966. The 1970 agreement won by the Maritime Administration was designed to overcome the present effects of past discriminatory initial placement decisions.

The most beneficial action seems to have been taken in the early 1970s, when the Tenneco management apparently decided that their access to federal contracting money would never again be jeopardized by the yard's racial practices.

Students of fair employment practices in the United States confess a dearth of experience in writing up successful cases. The Newport News Shipbuilding and Dry Dock Company is such a case, however. Table 3.5 provides numerical evidence to support this conclusion.

Blacks comprise 26 percent of the population in the labor-market area for the yard; hence, overall participation has never been a problem. Further, blacks held 43 percent of the skilled jobs by 1974.

By 1974 blacks held more than 32 percent of the office and clerical jobs, an important statistic considering that the first black clerical worker was hired in 1956.

As for blue-collar employment, the company was allowed in 1974 to eliminate its goals and timetables program for black males in all blue-collar operations except the electrical department, a highly unusual step.

In 1966, as Rubin pointed out, the yard had 32 black managers from a total of 1,997 managers (less than 2 percent).[14] By January 1974 the total number of managers had risen from roughly 2,000 to 3,000; blacks held 270 of these slots, or nearly 9 percent.

TABLE 3.5

Summary of EEO-1 Reports by Date Submitted, Newport News

	March 1971			February 1972			February 1973			January 1974		
	Total	Black	Percent Black	Total	Black	Percent Black	Total	Black	Percent Black	Total	Black	Percent Black
Managers	2,151	92	4.3	2,626	180	6.9	3,038	251	8.3	3,051	270	8.8
Professionals	2,932	46	1.6	3,126	91	2.9	3,513	128	3.6	3,408	159	4.7
Technical	1,112	60	5.4	1,410	137	9.7	2,100	247	11.8	1,473	265	17.9
Office	2,079	428	20.6	2,784	740	26.6	2,776	904	32.6	2,346	768	32.7
Skilled	6,742	2,177	32.3	6,953	2,484	35.7	8,565	3,603	42.1	8,011	3,488	43.5
Semiskilled	2,284	1,349	59.1	2,376	1,516	63.8	2,320	1,283	55.3	2,295	1,358	59.2
Laborers	823	449	54.6	4,184	2,434	58.2	3,576	2,100	58.7	2,971	1,471	49.5
Service	324	155	47.8	362	188	51.9	492	244	49.6	437	224	51.3
Total	18,447	4,756	25.8	23,821	7,770	32.6	26,380	8,760	33.2	23,992	8,003	33.4

Source: 1974 Affirmative Action Program for Equal Employment Opportunity at the Newport News Shipbuilding and Dry Dock Company, p. 48.

In March 1971 the yard employed 46 black professionals from a total professional population of 2,962 (less than 2 percent). The number of black professionals had risen to 159, or 4.7 percent of the total (3,408), by January 1974. Even though this appears low in relation to the total number of blacks in the labor market, it is perhaps not low considering the number of black professionals in the United States who are interested in and qualified to work in shipyards.

Black technicians comprised about 5.4 percent of the total in March 1971 but had increased to nearly 18 percent by January 1974.

In summary, by 1974 black participation in the Newport News labor force was not a problem. Nor was black participation in blue-collar employment, except for the electrical department. The yard's clerical work force was nearly 33 percent black. In addition, the rates of black participation among managers, professionals, and technicians were impressive.

It is very likely that the yard personnel department has encountered supply limitations in hiring black managers, professionals, and technicians. And although roughly 15 percent of those enrolled in the apprentice school are black, it is likely that the yard's extensive recruiting efforts have been hampered by supply limitations in this area as well.

While the yard has demonstrated an admirable EEO record with respect to blacks, the same can scarcely be said with respect to its recruitment of women. In the late 1960s the yard did begin to hire more and more women in blue-collar jobs (as did other shipyards across the country). However, this represents more of a breakthrough for women in one particular segment of the labor market than an indication of change across the board. The goals and timetables sections of the affirmative action plan for women make this clear. The yard is continuing its efforts to expand the work force of women in nontraditional occupations, but numerical success remains distant.

Although the yard's EEO efforts have been clear, some problems have arisen. Two examples will make this point.

The southern Virginia area has a history of segregation in its schools, and when the schools were finally integrated, a predictable controversy arose over the proportions of white and black teachers in the newly integrated faculties. Prior to integration, the area school faculties were approximately 39 percent black. Subsequent to integration, the faculties were roughly 29 percent black. Such a distribution led to a sizable number of unemployed black schoolteachers. It is likely that the school boards enforced credentials guidelines which fell disproportionately, but not surprisingly, on blacks.

In any event, the personnel office at the yard encountered high proportions of ex-schoolteachers applying for jobs—any jobs. These ex-schoolteachers had had far more education than most of the blue-collar employees at the yard, including those who had become supervisors in the operating and maintenance departments. In short, some employees with only a tenth-grade education were supervising others with college degrees.

This circumstance produced some morale problems at the yard. It also led the OCR to question the yard's personnel practices in regard to distribution of highly educated employees. The personnel office designed a form which college-educated employees were requested to sign, indicating that they understood the likely discrepancy between their own level of education and that of their supervisors.

Questioning by the OCR and the morale problems led to a harsh rule: no one with a college education would be allowed to take a job in the production or maintenance sections of the yard. This undoubtedly relieved some of the pressure on the yard EEO officer, but clearly such a policy reflected societal value judgments on blue-collar work and levels of education more than it did individual evaluation of employees.

A second problem is more serious in that its ramifications extended beyond the shipyard; it involves the history of black/white job designations and the problems which arise when an integration effort is initiated. There has been much discussion of the problems associated with the movement of "token" blacks into previously all-white departments. However, the Newport News experience provides insight into additional factors which must be considered.

When the yard decided to correct the inequities of its history, the personnel office developed a rule which was incorporated into the affirmative action plan. Put simply, if a department had less than 35 percent blacks, the proportion of black interviewees sent to that department was weighted to be high; conversely, if a department had over 35 percent blacks, the proportion of white interviewees sent to that department was weighted to be high. This latter policy caused several unforeseen difficulties.

The Newport News yard has about 24,000 employees. Most of these serve in blue-collar jobs in the production and maintenance departments. In order to preclude a wholesale shift of people within the yard, the personnel office formulated a fairly rigid transfer rule: The transfer must benefit both the employee and the yard. This means that the employee must be able to qualify for a higher grade through transfer than by remaining in his/her present department; the requirement that the transfer must also benefit the yard discourages movement of employees.

The yard has experienced some difficulty in retaining white employees in departments that are primarily black. Generally, after a few months on the job, white workers have requested transfers, complaining of harassment by blacks. Because of the strict enforcement of the transfer rule, many whites have quit their jobs when denied a transfer to another department.

Many of these predominantly black departments still have white supervisors. Because of the difficulty of retaining white employees in these units, the work force is likely to remain predominantly black. To counter the perpetuation of departments with white supervisors and black workers, the EEO officer has adopted a policy of promoting blacks into the foremen's and supervisors' jobs, reasoning that if white workers cannot be retained to eliminate the color line between workers and supervisors, then black supervisors may achieve that goal.[15] What this means, of course, is that the jobs (and departments) may become resegregated by this process.

Summary

The preceding evaluation of the efficacy of the federal government's enforcement efforts toward equal employment opportunity at the Newport News yard has been divided into four parts: the role of local labor-market pressures; the relationship between the Blumrosen and the Maritime Administration agreements and the pattern of overall change; the power of the federal government to influence racial employment patterns in this industry; and the role played by the Tenneco management in responding to pressure from the federal government.

The Newport News labor market seems to have escaped the high unemployment rates which plagued the rest of the United States after 1970. At one point the local authorities reported that the unemployment rate in the area had declined to only 2 percent. From 1966 to 1974, the total volume of employment at the yard was increasing (except for 1973–74), so the Newport News shipyard was seeking employees at a time when the labor market was generally acknowledged to be tight. Further, although the yard offered steady work, its pay scales were low compared to equivalent skills in other industries and its opportunities were for rough, dirty, and unpleasant positions, where the employees were often exposed to extremes of weather.

It could be argued that the increase in the black participation rate was due to labor-market pressures. However, it is questionable whether labor-market pressures produced black movement to foreman status or the changes in the number of blacks working as managers, professionals, and technicians.

The two agreements generated considerable hopeful anticipation and certainly promoted many rule changes. However, the numerical movement of blacks that can be attributed directly to these two battles is quite small for a yard that now employs about 24,000 persons.

A few promotions occurred because of the Blumrosen agreement, and a number of blacks were able to enter new lines of progression as a result of the changes demanded by the EEOC. The size of the affected class (1,835) in the June 1970 agreement concluded with the Maritime Administration suggests that many changes could have been effected. But by 1974 only 90 persons had completed the special training program, and 144 were still receiving training. Hence, our conclusion is that there is no numerical relationship between the two agreements and the successful EEO stance of the yard. As noted, the company brought about broad improvements in black participation in many job categories in the yard. It is readily apparent, however, that there is no connection between the number of persons affected and this account of the impact of the two settlements. What did occur was an aggressive and successful recruitment and promotion policy by the yard personnel office. Our focus is on how it took place.

First of all, there were many blacks available, both in the labor market area and employed at the yard. Second, the Maritime Administration group performed outstanding staff work. But the crucial factor in the change was a combination of government pressure and management response to that pressure.

The refusal of the Maritime Administration to release the funds for the laying of the keel of the nuclear aircraft carrier, the *Eisenhower*, convinced the Tenneco management that permanent changes had to be effected to eliminate the threat of contract cancellation or the delay of funds for any such project in the future.

INGALLS SHIPBUILDING DIVISION, LITTON INDUSTRIES

Pascagoula, Mississippi, is a small town at the mouth of the Pascagoula River on the Gulf of Mexico. For decades the natural harbor served as the base for a small shipbuilder, the Ingalls Iron Company. In the early 1960s the company was absorbed by Litton Industries, and its title was changed to the Ingalls Shipbuilding Division.

The original shipyard is known as the east-bank yard (since there is now a Litton-owned yard on the west bank as well). Soon after Litton bought the old yard, plans were made to construct a new facility to replicate the modular method of shipbuilding that has been used by the Japanese for the construction of supertankers. It took years to bring these plans to fruition.

One of the major problems was that the west bank needed a considerable amount of dredging before the yard could be built properly. Because dredging is both time-consuming and expensive, the Litton officials convinced the State of Mississippi that it was in the state's interest to prepare the waterway for the proposed new shipyard. The Mississippi legislature responded by passing a $130 million bond issue, and work began. Litton employees began to staff the yard in late 1969.

The old yard was organized by the Metal Trades Council, with nine constituent unions. The Litton management, feeling constrained by this organization, moved to keep its unions out of the west yard and established the new facility as a wholly independent subsidiary.

This move produced litigation which began before the NLRB and developed into a lengthy and costly process. The company eventually lost its fight with the union, and in May 1973 a single contract was signed between Litton and the Pascagoula Metal Trades Council for workers on both sides of the river.

One obvious reason for the lavish welcome for Litton by the State of Mississippi was the proposed number of jobs that would be available to Mississippi workers. These jobs did indeed become available, but some problems accompanied employment expansion in the town of Pascagoula. The projected increases in employment had an inflationary impact on land prices; the town faced a severe housing shortage; and workers had serious transportation difficulties in reaching the shipyards.

Further, although Litton has been very successful in obtaining both naval contracts and contracts to build ships for the U.S. commercial flag operations under subsidy from the Maritime Administration, the company has experienced some difficulties as a shipbuilder. Cost overruns and poor performance have led to vociferous criticism of Litton by some members of the Congress.

One result of this criticism was an internecine management fight at Litton. One of the issues involved was the extensive employment of aerospace engineers in the shipbuilding industry. As a conglomerate, Litton had extensive holdings in the West Coast aerospace industry. When the federal government cut back drastically on its outlay for Air Force hardware, Litton found that it had a surplus of aerospace engineers, many of whom were then transferred to the shipbuilding facility in Pascagoula. But the tolerances required for working with aluminum and those required for working with steel plate are considerably different, and eventually both a management team and a unit of aerospace engineers were dropped from the shipyard. The yard reverted to its previous style of management and integrated the management functions of its two locations.

All of these events occurred against the backdrop of changing race relations in the State of Mississippi. When Litton entered the area, the town and the shipyard were racially segregated. Thus, problems concerning the role of a civil rights employment enforcement bureaucracy took place in circumstances where there was a tremendous growth in the number of employees, a severe housing shortage and transportation problems, desegregation of the local school systems, opening up of public accommodations to all races, a management-union dispute which took years to settle, an internal fight among corporate managers, and heated criticism by powerful outsiders about the poor performance of the yard.

The yard is the major employer in Jackson County, so the level of economic activity in the county varies with employment in the yard. Further, unemployment in the county dropped at the beginning of the 1960s and remained around 3 percent for an eight-year period. Thus, the labor market for shipyard employees was extremely tight during the period of our interest, 1961–73 (see Table 3.6).

TABLE 3.6

Unemployment of the Civilian Labor Force, Jackson County, Mississippi, 1961-71

Year	Percent
Place of Residence Basis	
1961	10.6
1962	7.4
1963	4.4
1964	8.1
1965	3.2
1966	2.4
1967	2.4
1968	2.7
1969	2.4
1970	2.7
1971	4.4
Place of Work Basis	
1972	3.4
1973	3.2

Note: These data are observations for the month of January only. In a telephone interview with the manager of the Pascagoula branch of the Mississippi Employment Security Commission, it was confirmed that they reflect the general tightness of the local labor market.

Source: Annual Reports, Mississippi Employment Security Commission.

The Course of Events

The yard first felt the influence of federal government interest in its personnel practices in 1962, when staff members of the President's Committee on Equal Employment Opportunity arrived for an investigation. The only information available about this review suggests that although overt signs of segregated facilities at the yard were removed, virtually nothing was done about employment practices.[16] At that time, the yard had a black participation rate of about 5 percent in its work force.

Shortly after the initial contact by the President's Committee staff, compliance responsibility for the yard was assigned to the navy. Some changes were apparently made at that time in discriminatory placement patterns.[17] These were brought about through federal government funding.

Shortly after the Manpower Development and Training Act of 1962 was passed, the U.S. Department of Labor became interested in funding the yard (which had become the largest private employer in Mississippi) for training under the new legislation. This presented the personnel officials at the shipyard with a remarkable opportunity: They could have the federal government pay for training shipbuilders while at the same time moving blacks into the crafts via that training.

From the beginning, the yard's training classes were at least 30 percent black—the first break in the yard's previously segregated employment patterns in the skilled trades. The Metal Trades Council was inactive in these changes.

There have been civil rights protests about the practices of the yard, first in 1961 and again in 1964. The first was organized by longtime leader John LeFlore of Mobile, Alabama; the second was organized and led by Charles Evers, then head of the NAACP in Mississippi. It should be noted that both of these protests were organized by outsiders, reflecting the fact that the local black community was not well organized.

In 1968 the Department of Defense reorganized its EEO efforts, and the navy was relieved of compliance responsibility for the yard. The OCR was established and given compliance authority over coastal shipbuilding and ship repair.

In 1969 Order 4 was issued and the first affirmative action plan for the yard prepared. Although the enforcement agencies had developed the preaward clearance process by that time, in the spring of 1969 the navy let a multibillion-dollar contract to Litton without such clearance. This contract became the subject of a highly critical Senate speech by Ted Kennedy of Massachusetts.

The OCR was in the process of investigating the yard at the time, and some changes were made in the affirmative action plan. However, there was no agreement about any affected class as a whole, although goals and timetables were rewritten with the aim of eliminating underrepresentation by blacks in many crafts.

Following the passage of the 1964 Civil Rights Act, the EEOC began receiving charges against the yard by aggrieved individuals. Some of these were settled, but most languished in the agency's backlog of charges.

As late as 1968 the Painters Union, a member of the Metal Trades Council, had segregated locals. Neither unit was wholly white or wholly black, but the proportions were so decisive that the segregation was clear. The predominantly black local was confined primarily to the yard and was comprised of rust-machine operators, sandblasters, and similar workers.

Litton had cooperated with the Painters Union by dividing its lines of progression in the Paint Department to reflect the segregated nature of the locals in Pascagoula. When the Civil Rights Division and the Metal Trades Department of the AFL–CIO both ruled that the units should be merged immediately, Litton integrated the lines of progression by putting the black jobs into the bottom of the line that was organized by the predominantly white local. This achieved the result of giving the blacks the very worst jobs and the ones which fell at the bottom of the line of progression. In addition, blacks who chose were tested for certification as first-class painters; at least 15 were so certified.

There was no connection between the merged lines of progression, the first-class certification, and the affected-class settlement, but many of the blacks in the black local were considered members of the affected class.

There are two extremely important facets of the affected-class settlement in Pascagoula. First, the unions had a history of segregation that could have influenced blacks to vote against unionization or for other unions. Second, the company entered the settlement negotiations knowing that thousands of employees would be added to its rolls in the coming months.

The Metal Trades Council leadership realized that the unions were facing the threat of decertification because of their past racial policies. Following the passage of the 1964 Civil Rights Act, the council reviewed its black apprenticeship admission policies, and the first black apprentice was admitted to the Pascagoula Metal Trades Council in the spring of 1965.

The issue of race was omnipresent in Mississippi during the mid-1960s. Public accommodations were opened to all races at that time, and federal authorities moved to integrate the Mississippi public school systems. When the state AFL–CIO leadership endorsed integration of the schools, the Metal Trades Council in Pascagoula withdrew its membership in the state body. In addition, Mississippi has a "right-to-work" law, and many in the work force at Ingalls had strong reservations about unionism.

All of these factors combined to produce the fear of decertification; hence, the Metal Trades Council and other AFL–CIO affiliates became involved when the OCR moved to designate an affected class in the work force at Ingalls.

Negotiations for the affected-class settlement began in the spring of 1970; an agreement was signed on October 8, 1970. The government's effort was led by the OCR, with involvement by senior officials from Washington, D.C., and senior staff from the regional office in New Orleans. Ingalls was represented by its director of industrial relations, with assistance from its legal staff.

Officials of the local Metal Trades Council took part in the discussions and hired legal counsel for the duration of the negotiations. The leadership of the state AFL–CIO also participated.

But this was not all of the union involvement. Union officials at every level saw a threat to the seniority system and feared decertification. In Washington, D.C., the AFL–CIO Metal Trades Department and the Civil Rights Division reached an agreement to dispatch the deputy director of the Civil Rights Division to Pascagoula to assist in negotiating the affected-class settlement.

In addition, the AFL–CIO eventually supplemented its assistance by establishing a local unit of the Human Resources Development Institute in Pascagoula.

The Recruitment and Training Program was also invited to assist the metal trades unions in finding apprentices.

In the negotiations, the parties agreed to name 348 blacks who had been hired for certain jobs prior to July 1, 1966. These workers were classified as rust-machine operators, sandblasters, laborers, spray helpers, painters' helpers, and so on. Many of the class (but not a majority) were former members of the segregated painters local.

This remedy provided two avenues of relief for members of the affected class. The first involved promotion in a line of progression in the east yard; the other involved transfer to a line of progression in the new yard on the west bank. The sticking point in the negotiations was the provision, required by the OCR, that the members of the affected class would have carry-forward seniority; that is, they would take their previous yard seniority with them once they qualified for a position in the new line of progression.

The unions bargained for a face-saving clause in the settlement. Litton granted a provision specifying that no nonmember of the affected class would suffer unemployment or rate reduction as a result of benefits accruing to the members of the affected class. This was easy to concede, since growth projections for employment at the yard ran into the thousands, and Litton's estimate that this provision would cost nothing proved to be correct.

The agreement worked well. A compliance review dated April 12, 1973, stated: "Relief has been made available to all members of the class. Eighty-two percent . . . 286 of the original 348 Affected Class members have taken the relief options."[18] Table 3.7 shows the status of the members of the affected class as of December 1972.

Part of the union fear concerning decertification was manifest in the controversy over the ten-person Bi-Racial Committee which the yard established in 1966 without union involvement. The objective of this committee was to handle EEO problems before they went to outside agencies such as the EEOC or the OCR.

The five nonmanagement members of the committee were all black employees of the yard. Union officials suspected that management would use this committee to undermine the union—that Litton management would use the race issue to destroy the union at the yard.

The union's fear was so strong that one result of the negotiations was the establishment of Human Relations Committees on both sides of the river. Later, when the two yards were merged, the collective bargaining contract called for one Human Relations Committee for the entire yard. Although the clause remains in the contract, the committee has fallen into disuse, and there is no apparent interest by the membership in using this method to process grievances.

The Bi-Racial Committee had only advisory authority in the cases brought before it. Management representatives failed to attend and sent low-echelon alternates in their place. When a personality conflict developed between the

TABLE 3.7

Status of the Affected Class at Ingalls, December 15, 1972

Current Status	Numbers[a]
Transferred to the new yard	98
Promoted	153
Separated	51
No change[b]	46
Total	348

[a]The first choices of the members of the affected class resulted in 97 transfers to the new yard and 189 promotions at the old yard for a total of 286 actions out of 348 possible choices. However, some of these retired, died, or were fired. Six were demoted, and two of the transfers to the east yard returned to their old duty stations. Seven members who were originally promoted in the east yard transferred to the west yard.

[b]These employees did not apply for transfer or promotion.

Source: Report filed by OCR, New Orleans, dated April 12, 1973.

elected head of the committee and the other members, the director of the regional OCR intervened.

The OCR wanted the committee restaffed and restructured, with some power to effect remedies. These negotiations took place in the spring of 1973. Management agreed to place high-echelon executives on the committee and gave the committee enforcement power. An appeal mechanism was designed where the losing party could appeal the decision of the committee to the chief executive officer of the yard. Finally, the controversial elected head of the committee agreed to step down.

The Bi-Racial Committee, now renamed the Affirmative Action Committee, operates as a mini-EEOC. It hears and investigates complaints, and it can order any of the standard Title VII remedies except back pay. Considering its previous lack of enforcement power, these provisions are truly a step forward.

One official at the yard estimates that about 60 to 65 percent of the yard's EEO complaints come to the committee. Hence, it serves the function of reducing the work load which would otherwise devolve to the EEOC or the OCR in New Orleans. However, many union officials refuse to encourage their members to use the committee, usually dismissing it with the caveat that "only company men sit on that committee."[19]

Growth and Change in Southern Mississippi

For many years federal officials who work on employment discrimination efforts have used a benchmark for comparison against an employer's performance, usually the percentage of a minority in the local population or in the local labor force. In Pascagoula, OCR staff and Litton personnel have been unable to agree on an appropriate benchmark.

Order 4 made it necessary for government contractors to file affirmative action plans. Further, it was necessary for the government contractor to specify the minority and sex content of the labor force drawn upon. The usual procedure by the contractor involves relying on two sources: the decennial census and labor-market reports issued by state employment agencies.

These two sources have been acceptable to the Office of Federal Contract Compliance. However, the contractor and the compliance agency may disagree about the geographic size of the contractor's labor market, and such was the case in Pascagoula.

When the first affirmative action plan for Ingalls was filed, the report identified five counties in southern Mississippi as the appropriate labor-market area; those counties yielded a black percentage (of the population) of about 16 percent. The company used this percentage as its relative benchmark.

The OCR, however, disagreed; specifically, it claimed that all of Mobile County, Alabama, should also be included, which would have raised the benchmark. The OCR staff also wanted to add some counties in Mississippi without hesitation. Such is the influence of economic growth.

This issue was resolved by hard bargaining. The OCR agreed that Ingalls should be allowed to survey the work force to determine its residence. The result was that the western half of Mobile County was included in the labor market area; since this portion of the county had the same percentage of blacks as the original five-county area, however, there was no change in the benchmark. The additional counties in Mississippi were not added.

The issue was brought up again when Litton began to staff the west-bank facility at Ingalls. The staff in the OCR convinced Litton personnel that recruitment should be conducted "nationally" for some jobs and that a different mix of counties should be used. Hence, the benchmark for the west yard came to be 18.7 percent, while that for the east yard was 16.4 percent (as it had been from the filing of the first affirmative action plan).

By the time the parties agreed on these benchmarks, the yards had been merged, but Litton refused to bargain for just one benchmark. The issue became moot, however, since by the time negotiations were concluded, minority percentages at the combined yards exceeded both benchmarks. Hence, overall participation of blacks in yard employment is no longer an issue.

Participation in particular crafts remained in controversy, however. In the Ingalls yard (as in the others studied), craftsmen listed in the EEO-1 reports

TABLE 3.8

Black Craftsmen at Ingalls, 1969-73

Year	West Bank		East Bank		Combined Yard	
	Number	Percent of Total	Number	Percent of Total	Number	Percent of Total
1969			286	6.4		
1970	11	5.5	269	8.6		
1971	138	9.7	356	10.9		
1972	344	13.7	481	13.9		
1973					1,212	20.3

Source: EEO-1 forms.

TABLE 3.9

Black Operatives at Ingalls, 1969-73

Year	West Bank		East Bank		Combined Yard	
	Number	Percent of Total	Number	Percent of Total	Number	Percent of Total
1969			523	31.0		
1970	55	28.4	520	37.0		
1971	372	24.6	600	32.0		
1972	736	31.5	768	36.0		
1973					2,167	40.0

Source: EEO-1 forms.

were almost exclusively the mechanics in the various trades. Table 3.8 shows that in 1970 both yards had very low percentages of black craftsmen (8.6 percent for the east yard, 5.5 percent for the west yard). However, by 1973 the combined yards showed participation at 20 percent.

The Ingalls yard, like the others studied, trains many of its shipbuilders. Hence, the large reservoir of blacks who are classified as operatives and as eligible for on-the-job training that will lead to the craftsman classification is significant. Table 3.9 indicates the relatively high percentage of blacks holding these jobs in the yard, but the important statistic is that there were over 2,100 blacks in the pipeline in late 1973.

TABLE 3.10

Black Clericals at Ingalls, 1969-73

Year	West Bank		East Bank		Combined Yard	
	Number	Percent of Total	Number	Percent of Total	Number	Percent of Total
1969			104	12.5		
1970	50	14.8	73	18.0		
1971	55	14.8	58	17.6		
1972	90	20.4	65	19.0		
1973					229	22.0

Source: EEO-1 forms.

Black clerical workers are shown for both yards and the combined yards in Table 3.10. The overall number is rather low, but the percentage of blacks holding these jobs approaches the overall black participation rate at the yard. This is rather unusual—especially for a deep-South employer—and warrants further attention in the following section.

Table 3.11 illustrates the overall status of all minorities in the combined yards as of late 1973. Our interest centers on the top three classifications and their minority percentages: officials and managers, 6.6 percent; professionals, 6.5 percent; and technicians, 11.8 percent. These are the highest percentages for these classifications that have ever been achieved at the Ingalls yard.

It is difficult to project when supply limitations will operate to restrict available black workers for these classifications, but it can be argued that it will take a considerable amount of time to double the present percentages. The number of minorities with the education and training for these jobs is obviously low at present. Second, it is unlikely that shipyards will be as willing as many other employers to pay premiums for minority professionals, technicians, and managers. Third, it is also likely that minorities with the requisite skills who are willing to live in the deep South will decide that the shipbuilding industry offers fewer opportunities than other industries for developing their potential.

Remaining Issues

The Ingalls yard has accomplished some meaningful changes in overall placement of minorities, and the affected-class settlement was negotiated well on the whole, but some issues remain which require discussion: the placement of

TABLE 3.11

East and West Yards Combined, Ingalls, 1973

Job Title	Total	Males	Females	Minorities*								Total Minorities	Percent of Total That Is Minority
				Males				Females					
				B	O	AI	SSA	B	O	AI	SSA		
Officials and managers	1,923	1,881	42	113	0	7	0	8	0	0	0	128	6.6
Professionals	2,494	2,348	146	130	3	4	0	26	0	1	0	164	6.5
Technicians	1,220	1,078	142	112	0	3	0	28	0	1	0	144	11.8
Sales	0	0	0	0	0	0	0	0	0	0	0	0	0
Office and clerical	1,043	94	949	28	0	1	0	201	1	2	0	233	22.3
Craftsmen	5,976	5,860	116	1,135	3	20	0	77	0	0	0	1,235	20.7
Operatives	5,412	4,755	657	1,768	0	65	0	399	0	12	0	2,244	41.5
Laborers	572	427	145	263	0	0	0	105	0	3	0	371	64.9
Service workers	262	170	92	39	0	1	0	39	1	0	0	79	30.2
Totals	18,902	16,613	2,289	3,588	6	101	0	883	1	19	0	4,598	24.3

* B = Black; O = Oriental; AI = American Indian; SSA = Spanish-surnamed American.

Source: EEO–1 form for combined yard, December 1973.

91

TABLE 3.12

Female Blue-Collar and Total Blue-Collar Employees at Ingalls, 1973

Job Title	Females			Total Employees	Female/ Total
	Black	Anglo	Total		
Craftsmen	77	39	116	5,976	1.94
Operatives	399	258	657	5,412	12.14
Laborers	105	40	145	572	25.34
Totals	581	337	918	11,960	7.68

Source: Table 3.11.

women in blue-collar jobs, the placement of black women in low-level clerical jobs, and the contribution of the outreach-type agencies.

The blue-collar jobs reported on the EEO-1 form fall into three categories: craftsmen, operatives, and laborers. The combined yards in December 1973 employed nearly 12,000 persons in these blue-collar jobs, of whom 918, or 7.7 percent, were women. In 1969 no women had been employed in these classifications. Table 3.12 shows the exact number so employed in 1973.

In other yards women have broken through traditional sex barriers to acquire these jobs, but the Ingalls yard represents a deliberate and determined effort to recruit and place women in such classifications. Litton's policy in this regard is a replica of the American World War II experience with one important difference: The change in personnel policy is intended to be permanent.

Earlier it was noted that the percentage of black clerical workers exceeded the benchmark figure agreed on by the yard and the OCR. However, these overall rates mask a potentially explosive issue.

Interviews revealed that many of the office and clerical jobs—although classified as white-collar work—are of a low-level clerical nature. The company may have decided to fill these jobs with blacks to improve its EEO position.

However, it also appears that the company has not constructed a line of progression that would allow the entrants to move to higher grades in the white-collar classifications. This possibility was investigated by staff in the OCR while making an on-site review, and their eventual conclusion was that increasing the percentage of black clerical workers is an admirable goal, but if it is accomplished in such a way that employees in these jobs cannot progress to other classifications, and if a disproportionate number of these employees are black, then the company may be creating an affected class. The example cited was a unit which cut, folded, and filed blueprints.

An additional issue raised by the progression difficulty cited above is whether it may be a mistake to use the Mississippi State Employment Service for testing potential clerk-typists. The employment service uses a cutoff point of 55 words per minute with a maximum of five mistakes to certify eligibility for clerk-typist jobs, yet this level of typing skill is rarely required in many jobs at the yard. Although such levels of skill are rarely required, however, failure to use them for entry requirements may create, as noted with the blueprint group, an affected class of employees who are prevented from moving into higher classifications.

The argument is not that entry-level clerical workers must be prepared to become executive directors but rather that the company should design its entry-level requirements to fit the needs of its lines of progression. It is common and accepted practice to establish pyramid-like job structures, with the clear implication that not all low-level employees must be qualified for promotion. The point is simply that the entry-level requirements should coincide with the total needs of the lines of progression in which entrants will be placed. Thus the typing test used by the employment service may not necessarily be discriminatory; in fact, it may be considered a legitimate business necessity. (OCR staff have charged that the Mississippi State Employment Service administers the typing test unfairly, but this is a separate issue subject to separate legal prosecution.)

The Contribution of Outreach

The Pascagoula yard has received some assistance in its massive recruitment tasks from two outreach organizations: the Recruitment and Training Program and the Human Resources Development Institute (HRDI). Both of these groups began to function in Pascagoula during the spring of 1971.

HRDI is a two-person unit which has concentrated its efforts on bringing ex-convicts still on parole into the shipyard. Although the total number of placements was not revealed to the researcher on this project, the overall numbers involved are quite small.

RTP began with a small staff, but in early 1974 the staff was increased to eight people. This unit has worked at bringing people (with no restrictions related to race or sex) into the yard as apprentices in indenture programs or as helpers in a line of progression.

From 1971 through March 31, 1976, the Pascagoula RTP office reported a total of 1,615 placements, which fell into the classifications shown in Table 3.13. Although data on placement characteristics were not conveniently available on activity before September 15, 1975, information for the period from that date through March 31, 1976, is indicative of RTP's performance.

TABLE 3.13

Placements by RTP at Ingalls, 1971–March 31, 1976

Job Classification	Number	As a Percent of Total
Construction apprentices	13	.8
Other skilled construction workers	17	.1
Industrial apprentices	113	7
Industrial journeymen	137	8
Other skilled industrial workers	822	51
Other occupations	513	32

Source: Calculated from RTP reports filed with the U.S. Department of Labor.

Data for the 740 placements made during that nine-month period indicate that 34 percent were female and 70 percent were black. Moreover, more than 99 percent were reported placed at jobs earning $3.00 or more per hour. Prior to placement, 66 percent had been earning less than $3.00 per hour.

Although the data are not conclusive, they do tend to show that the RTP outreach program in Pascagoula made a substantial number of placements, especially after 1974. Further, it appears that a majority of the placements have been black and that a significant portion have been female; in addition, the project has effected notable upgrading for its placements.

Summary

This evaluation of the federal government's enforcement efforts in Pascagoula, Mississippi, can be considered in four parts: the impact of labor-market pressures, the relationship between the affected-class settlement and the growth in employment, the role played by the local unions and their federations, and the exercise of surveillance by the federal government.

Jackson County, where the Litton yard is located, has experienced tremendous growth in the number of persons employed. This has been a steady trend since the early 1960s. This can be considered largely a function of shipyard employment, especially after staffing of the west-bank facility.

Along with the increase in employment has come an extremely low annual unemployment rate, about 3 percent or less. The yard has attracted employees from distant areas, so there is no question about the tightness of the labor market. The capacity of the labor force is further strained by the Ingalls yard's high rate of voluntary terminations. As one management official said, "We have cut turnover nine different ways, and we still suffer from it."[20]

In any event, there is no doubt that the Ingalls yard has been active in recruiting—so active, in fact, that the OCR staff in New Orleans was apparently arguing a moot point in trying to determine the correct size of the labor market to be used as the basis for a benchmark.

Much of the increase in the number of minorities working at the yard is obviously a combination of Litton's demand and the availability of such workers in the area surrounding the facility. As in many places, economic growth has apparently been the ingredient which has facilitated social change in southeastern Mississippi.

It would be difficult to cite a better example of the contribution of economic growth toward social change than the affected-class settlement negotiated by the participants in Pascagoula. During the process of negotiations it was clear to all parties that the number of new hires would increase by the thousands in the subsequent few months. In addition, since the affected class numbered no more than 348 members, even if all of these were moved, they could be distributed among eight other constituent unions belonging to the Metal Trades Council and the IBEW local. Hence, no union would receive a large number of members of the affected class.

But economic growth allowed more than that. The parties agreed under pressure from union officials that nonmembers of the affected class employed before a certain date would suffer neither unemployment nor a rate reduction as a consequence of rights afforded to the affected class. This guarantee remained in effect for two years. It will be noted in the following section that the Alabama Dry Dock Company balked unconditionally at a similar proviso in its affected-class settlement, yet at Litton agreement on this issue was reached without hesitation. Such is the influence of economic growth.

Earlier it was stated that the increase in the number of minorities at the yard could be attributed to the twin influences of demand by Litton and the availability of blacks and other minorities. Other pressures also account for the upgrading of minorities working at the yard.

Prior to passage of the Civil Rights Act of 1964, no black had ever served as an indentured apprentice at the yard; in the spring of 1965, the first black entered an indenture program at the yard. When the affected-class negotiations began in 1970, the issue of token minority participation in the crafts also arose. Simultaneously, unions at all levels encouraged the work of the RTP, and the AFL–CIO—with monetary help from the Manpower Administration—established the HRDI unit in Pascagoula.

Most important, the training facilities at the yard have been opened to all applicants. The unions and the company have reversed themselves on this issue, with the help of the OCR in New Orleans. In the context of an accelerated growth in numbers, this reversal has produced some problems.

During the first part of 1974, the yard had about 1,400 indentured apprentices. The director of training indicated in an interview at that time that there were too many apprentices going through the programs. The same observation was voiced later in the year by the director of the RTP operation.

Their reasoning was similar: the proportions of journeymen, apprentices, and helpers were so out of kilter that it was impossible to rotate the apprentices as required by the rules of the joint apprenticeship committees (each apprentice is required to work a specified number of weeks with journeymen on different tasks so that by the end of a certain time the apprentice can be tested on all aspects of the trade). Laudable efforts at training large numbers of would-be shipbuilders were apparently diluting the quality of the training. As a result, an effort was made to cut back on the intake of new apprentices by reducing the maximum age requirement from 24 (where it had been for many years) to 22.

This solution raises another potential conflict. Because of the history of their past exclusion at the yard, young minorities who have had very limited access to the indentured training programs because of their race may suffer a "disparate effect" from the reduction of the entry age. This is undoubtedly true, but under the argument of business necessity, the case can also be made that the training facility is currently overloaded, deleteriously affecting the quality of training.

It may be that the parties will have to work out a solution with two effects: reduction of the number of new apprentices on the grounds of business necessity, and use of a criterion or set of criteria which does not produce a disparate effect on minority and female applicants. This example demonstrates the need for continuing surveillance.

The federal government has provided more than continuing surveillance; Litton has been a successful negotiator for federal government contracts. The company was also successful in negotiating the expenditure of $130 million by the state of Mississippi for a dredging operation to support a major shipbuilding installation on the west bank. Shipbuilding depends on government (federal and state) money, and that kind of dependence enhances the power of compliance agencies.

It is difficult to avoid the conclusion that the pattern of overall change requires more than a labor-market explanation. The movement of minorities into the pipeline for upgrading to mechanic status, the active recruitment of minorities into indentured apprenticeships, and the changing racial proportions of the clerical work force are all indications of a deliberate response to the prodding of the staff in the OCR. The number of women in blue-collar classifications is a manifestation of civil rights pressure (see Table 3.12). The conclusion is clear: The upgrading afforded minorities and women is seen as the price for continued access to federal government money.

ALABAMA DRY DOCK AND SHIPBUILDING COMPANY

The Alabama Dry Dock and Shipbuilding Company was founded in the early 1920s. The yard had approximately 2,900 employees in 1974. At the peak of shipbuilding activity during World War II, the yard employed some 30,000 workers. However, it is now primarily a repair facility.

Since World War II, the company has constructed two vessels for the U.S. Navy and in 1974 was under contract to construct floating offshore oil-drilling platforms. The dominant activity of the yard, however—and that which has most heavily influenced the content of its labor-management relations—is ship repair work.

Ship repair work is unpredictable, often calling for large numbers of employees on short notice. Many of the yard's workers have thus adjusted their life styles to the erratic nature of the call-in/layoff activity at the yard (in the past, many regular employees were small farmers who held second jobs at the yard). The most important adjustment to the volatile nature of employment at the yard, however, has been the insistence on craft seniority in the collective bargaining contract.

The collective bargaining contract is between the company and Local 18 of the Industrial Union of Marine and Shipbuilding Workers of America. Although this is an industrial union, it is extremely craft-conscious. In fact, the raison d'être of the union has been its ability to protect its members' employment rights against those who have less time in an occupation or unit. Until very recently (except for noncompetitive benefits), no such thing as yard seniority existed.

The Actors and the Environment

In December 1973, Judge Hand of the U.S. District Court in Mobile issued a consent decree worked out by the parties after lengthy discussions, debate, and at times acrimonious exchanges. There were several actors in this drama: the management of the company, the attorneys for the company, Local 18 of the union and its attorneys, the OCR, an assistant secretary of commerce, attorneys for the EEOC, the OFCC in the U.S. Department of Labor, and two local civil rights organizations—the NAACP and the Non-Partisan Voters League.

As noted previously, in mid-1968 the compliance function for coastal shipbuilding and ship repair, formerly handled by the OFCC under Executive Order 11246, was shifted from the Department of Defense and the navy to the OCR. In 1969, Order 4 under the executive order became effective, and the contractors covered by the order were compelled to submit acceptable affirmative action plans. The submission of the 1970 affirmative action plan by the Alabama

Dry Dock and Shipbuilding Company was the beginning of the drama which culminated in Judge Hand's acceptance of a consent decree in December 1973.

The Mobile Economy

The Mobile SMSA is comprised of Mobile and Baldwin Counties. The total population was 363,389 in 1960, growing to 376,690 in 1970. Blacks totaled about 30 percent of the population in both census years. The best estimate is that this percentage approached 31 or 32 percent by 1975. Spanish-surnamed Americans and people listed under "other races" account for no more than 1 percent of the total population.

The local economy is extremely diversified; there is no one dominant industry or sector. The wage and salary labor force grew slowly—about 1 percent per year—from 1960 through 1973. The civilian labor force in the SMSA has shown a slight increase (see Table 3.14).

The overall unemployment rate from 1960 through 1973 fluctuated around 5 percent. Blacks represent approximately 25 percent of the employed civilian labor force but are burdened with roughly 40 percent of the area's unemployment.

The local labor market has had sufficient slack in it that the Alabama Dry Dock Company could tap ample numbers of potential new employees, even though it pays lower wages than competitive employers. (The average weekly wage for shipbuilders and ship repair workers was about $10 per week below the average weekly wage for all manufacturing employees in the same area.)

TABLE 3.14

Mobile SMSA Civilian Labor Force and Annual Rates of Unemployment, 1970-73

Year	Civilian Labor Force (in thousands)	Rate of Unemployment (percent)
1970	139	4.5
1971	139.3	5.6
1972	142.6	5.2
1973	149.7	4.3

Source: Mobile: Metropolitan Area—Area Manpower Review (Mobile: Alabama Department of Industrial Relations, Alabama State Employment Service, August 1974), p. 23.

The Course of Events

The filing of an affirmative action plan in 1970 by the Alabama Dry Dock Company set the stage for ensuing action. The OCR found the affirmative action plan deficient. The yard exhibited a classic pattern of assigning jobs on the basis of race and further restricting movement by blacks into certain lines of progression and certain departments.

After the 1970 affirmative action plan was rejected, OCR staff and industrial relations personnel at the Alabama Dry Dock Company worked out a supplemental agreement. The major concept adopted in this agreement was the definition of an affected class, which was said to include all blacks hired for certain jobs before July 1, 1966. The parties agreed that initial discriminatory assignments had stopped after that date.

The relief specified that members of the affected class were to be allowed to move into different departments and to enter lines of progression leading to the third-class mechanic jobs. From that slot, employees could move to second- and first-class status.

The union agreed to the plan, which was then forwarded to Washington, D.C., for review. The reviewing officials in the OFCC, however, rejected the supplemental agreement, which was then returned to the Maritime Administration with instructions to increase the size of the affected class and to give more options to the relief provided for the affected class.

Negotiations between the Maritime Administration and the Alabama Dry Dock Company were reopened. As these discussions continued, Maritime Administration officials began to threaten to debar the company as a government contractor. In late January 1971, the Department of Commerce formally notified the company that it could not bid on new government contracts.

The company responded on February 10, 1971, asking for a hearing and arguing that no action should be taken against it until the hearing process had been completed. A hearing was granted, but the sanctions remained in effect. The company's argument was that it could not accept the Maritime Administration's amended supplemental agreement because the union demanded protection for any members who might be adversely affected by the rights won for affected-class members.

In April 1971 the government enumerated various charges against the company and concluded, as anticipated, by asking for debarment. This set in motion a number of actions by attorneys for the company, Local 18 and the national union, and the Department of Commerce.

While the attorneys were filing and answering interrogatories and exchanging stipulations of facts, OCR officials and company staff were trying to negotiate an amended supplemental agreement. At the same time (summer of 1971), the navy began to act on its own.

Some time earlier the navy had leased a floating dry dock to the company, which had been used for performing repair work. After its contract expired during the course of preparations for the hearing, the navy refused to extend the lease, and the dry dock was floated away. This was an additional blow to the yard, since the sanctions against them prohibited bidding for additional government contracts. There is no proof that the navy's action was related to the EEO practices of the yard, but officials of the company and the union are so convinced. Total employment at the yard dropped by about 1,400 jobs, and the yard was, as one official said, "crying for compliance."

An amended supplemental agreement was worked out, but the union refused to assent to it without a clause protecting members who did not belong to the affected class. The company considered this to be a "feather-bedding" demand and accordingly rejected it. The result was that the company and Maritime Administration personnel faced the draft of yet another document.

A second amended supplemental agreement was drafted and accepted by the company and the union on February 23, 1972. However, the company and the Maritime Administration entered into an additional agreement on March 15, 1972, which incorporated and modified the February 23, 1972, agreement. The modification involved the use of carry-forward seniority for members of the affected class.

The union objected to this section of the package and on April 4, 1972, filed suit, charging the company with breach of contract. In the fall of 1972 the suit was amended to add as defendants the secretary of labor and the secretary of commerce, who maintain responsibility for enforcing Executive Order 11246.

Meanwhile, workers at the yard had filed charges with the EEOC, which consolidated 43 complaints and asked for a conciliation conference. This began prior to the acceptance of the Maritime Administration package in March 1972 and continued subsequent to it.

On December 12, 1972, the company and the EEOC disposed of the 43 complaints with a conciliation agreement which incorporated the March 15, 1972, Maritime Administration settlement, added back pay for some charging parties, and gave preference for some jobs to members of the affected class over certain employees who—under the Maritime Administration agreement—would have had priority over members of the affected class.

The union then added the EEOC as a defendant to its breach-of-contract suit. The general counsel for the EEOC responded by filing a separate suit, under the authority of the 1972 amendments, against Local 18.

Neither the hearing nor the breach-of-contract trial took place. All parties worked out a consent decree, filed on December 27, 1973, which had several parts: the second amended supplemental agreement, the Maritime Administration settlement, the EEOC-company conciliation agreement, and two appendixes which specified some limited protection for employees who were not members of the affected class who might suffer "economic harm" as a result of the

Maritime Administration and EEOC agreements. In addition, the EEOC dropped its lawsuit against the union, and the company agreed to pay the union's legal costs.

The Affected-Class Settlement

The affected-class settlement flows from three documents: the second amended supplemental agreement, the Maritime Administration agreement of March 15, 1972, and parts of the EEOC conciliation agreement. The movement (or lack of it) of members of the affected class can be evaluated with reference to Tables 3.15 and 3.16.

The affected class was composed of 304 black employees hired prior to July 1, 1966, in 18 different occupations. Relief was provided in one of two forms: a promotion program or a handyman program.

The company had denied blacks promotional opportunities in some departments and jobs in other departments and agreed, under the terms of the consent decree, to examine the qualifications of members of the affected class in the jobs where they were currently working. A total of 37 employees had been promoted under this program by the end of 1974. Ten members of the affected class were permanent foremen in their original departments. Twenty-seven had received promotions to mechanic, groundsman, material checker, and other classifications, all in the original departments of the members of the affected class. Wages were not "red-circled" (see glossary).

TABLE 3.15

Current Status of Members of the Affected Class at Alabama Dry Dock Who Moved, September 1974

New Jobs	Promotion Program*	Handyman Program
Permanent foreman	10	
Mechanic (including groundsmen, material checkers, etc.)	27	20
Helpers		5
Handyman (currently in training)		6
Totals	37	31 = 68

*Those who benefited from the promotion program remained in their original department.

Source: Report on Maritime Administration Settlement dated September 17, 1974.

TABLE 3.16

Disposition of Members of the Affected Class at Alabama Dry Dock Who Did Not Move, September 1974

Reason	Number
Declined to exercise option to move	156
Declined to move after first expressing a preference to move	18
Disqualified or voluntarily dropped out after starting training	6
Disqualified by company before starting training	2
Did not participate: terminated, deceased or retired	54
Total	236

Source: Report on the Maritime Administration Settlement dated September 17, 1974.

The handyman program was basically an on-the-job training program for members of the affected class. In most cases, the handyman was slotted between helper and third-class mechanic in lines of progression; in cases where there were no helpers in a department, the handyman was slotted at the bottom of the line.

The handyman classification was divided into two parts: first class and second class. The agreement specified that the affected-class member would work 720 hours in each part and if qualified would be promoted to third-class mechanic at the end of 1,440 hours. A provision was made for transferees who failed to qualify for third-class mechanic status but who wished to remain in their new departments as helpers with yard seniority (if they were so qualified).

Some kind of upgrading resulted from the program for 20 workers (see Table 3.15). Five transferees remained in the training phase of the program. Everyone who moved under the handyman program did so with a red-circled rate. However, the red-circled rate was limited to the rate paid the top non-supervisory employee in the line for which the employee trained.

A high proportion of the affected class did not move initially or failed to move for various reasons after first indicating a preference for movement. If it is assumed that the six people still in training are successful, then 68 of the 304 (or 22 percent) in the affected class benefited from the program. As shown in Table 3.16, more than half of the affected class declined to exercise their option to move.

The Overall Magnitude of Recent Change

Table 3.17 gives the standard breakdown by race and sex for nine job titles used by both the OFCC and the EEOC. In 1964 the Alabama Dry Dock Company presented almost a classic picture of a discriminator.

For instance, every official, manager, professional, and technician was a white male. Every laborer was a black male. Every maid was a black female.

TABLE 3.17

Modified EEO-1 Form, Alabama Dry Dock, 1964

Job Title	Total Employment	Males		Females	
		Total	Blacks	Total	Blacks
Officials and managers	31	31	0	0	0
Professionals	35	35	0	0	0
Technicians	73	73	0	0	0
Office and clerical	109	45	6	64	0
Sales	1	1	0	0	0
Journeymen and mechanics	1,519	1,517	162	2	0
Semiskilled	676	676	290	0	0
Laborers	124	124	124	0	0
Service workers	42	36	3	6	6
Totals	2,610	2,538	585	72	6

Source: SF 41, Part I, Section E dated October 27, 1964.

There were, however, two female journeyman mechanics at that time. While blacks held only 22 percent of the jobs at the company in 1964, they comprised 30 percent of the population of the Mobile SMSA and nearly 25 percent of the civilian labor force.

Between 1964 and 1970 (see Table 3.18), the volume of employment at the yard shot up by some 1,400 employees, and apparently most of this increase took place between 1969 and 1970.

Some token changes took place in the upper echelons: eight blacks became officials, managers, professionals, and technicians, and eight black females worked in the office and clerical category (see Table 3.18). By 1970 the formerly all-black male laborer category had been integrated by the addition of 35 white males, but the unit remained an all-male preserve.

It is interesting to note that while the black participation rate stayed almost level between 1969 and 1970 (see Tables 3.17 and 3.18)—a period of increasing employment—the same rate actually increased in the context of declining yard employment between 1970 and 1973 (see Tables 3.18 and 3.19).

It is likely that these changes reflect a growing uneasiness by the union and the company about the pattern of past placement on the grounds of race. This general uneasiness was apparently replaced by genuine concern in the period after 1970.

Evidence supporting the contention that the yard made an effort to comply with EEO directives includes three points: the racial composition of new hires between 1970 and 1974 (see Table 3.20) and of recent promotions into all classes of the mechanic title (see Table 3.21); the increased number of women in blue-collar occupations by 1974 (see Table 3.20); and the number of black foremen in several departments.

TABLE 3.18

Modified EEO-1 Form, Alabama Dry Dock, 1970

Job Title	Total Employment	Males		Females	
		Total	Blacks	Total	Blacks
Officials and managers	102	101	2	1	0
Professionals	90	81	4	9	0
Technicians	36	32	2	4	1
Sales	1	1	0	0	0
Office and clerical	165	86	2	79	8
Craftsmen	2,591	2,591	418	0	0
Operatives	876	876	338	0	0
Laborers	203	203	168	0	0
Service workers	42	36	11	6	6
Totals	4,106	4,007	945[a]	99	15[a]
Previous year's totals	2,757	2,644	659[b]	93	11[b]

[a]Black participation rate for 1970 = 23.4 percent.
[b]Black participation rate for 1969 = 24.3 percent.
Source: Payroll for Alabama Dry Dock, April 16, 1970.

TABLE 3.19

Modified EEO-1 Form, Alabama Dry Dock, 1973

Job Title	Total Employment	Males		Females	
		Total	Blacks	Total	Blacks
Officials and managers	77	75	1	2	0
Professionals	71	67	7	4	0
Technicians	33	27	3	6	1
Sales	1	1	0	0	0
Office and clerical	108	48	5	60	7
Craftsmen	1,536	1,530	333	6	4
Operatives	510	510	280	0	0
Laborers	261	261	202	0	0
Service workers	44	40	14	4	4
Totals	2,641	2,559	845[a]	82	16*

*Black participation rate for 1973 = 32.6 percent.
Source: EEO-1 form dated March 5, 1973.

TABLE 3.20

Modified EEO-1 Form, Alabama Dry Dock, 1974

Job Title	Total Employment	Males		Females	
		Total	Blacks	Total	Blacks
Officials and managers	75	73	1	2	0
Professionals	76	68	4	8	0
Technicians	41	35	3	6	1
Sales	1	1	0	0	0
Office and clerical	120	51	5	69	9
Craftsmen	1,747	1,736	385	11	5
Operatives	632	628	339	4	2
Laborers	200	200	166	0	0
Service workers	42	36	14	6	6
Totals	2,934	2,829	917	105	23

Source: EEO-1 Form dated January 17, 1974.

TABLE 3.21

Employment of Mechanics by Race, Alabama Dry Dock, 1970 and 1973

	First-Class Mechanics	Second-Class Mechanics	Third-Class Mechanics	Total Mechanics
1970				
Total	593	643	1,314	2,550
Black	19	44	95	158
White	574	599	1,219	2,392
Percent black	3.20	6.84	7.23	6.20
Percent white	96.80	93.16	92.77	93.80
1973				
Total	374	388	601	1,363
Black	26	78	174	278
White	348	310	427	1,085
Percent black	6.95	20.10	28.95	20.40
Percent white	93.05	79.90	71.05	79.60

Source: Hiring reports, Alabama Dry Dock Company.

The data in Table 3.21 require elucidation on one key point. The Alabama Dry Dock yard is a repair yard and as such has considerable call-in/layoff activity. Further, the data compiled in Table 3.21 represent both new hires and recalls. It is axiomatic among civil rights enforcement officials that recruitment from the same pool which produced discriminatory patterns earlier is suspect, if not illegal. One yard official indicated that "fully 80 percent of our new hires [and recalls] on a monthly basis are former employees," suggesting that the past pattern would be perpetuated.

Thus, it is comforting to note the changes between 1970 and 1974, particularly the higher proportion of blacks employed during that period. Further, the data in Table 3.21 are for mechanics only. The Alabama Dry Dock experience has to be considered an example of affirmative recruitment, even if the 80 percent figure noted above might have implied otherwise.

If the recent hiring pattern suggests that the yard can and will find blacks to hire in craft classifications, it is also true that recent promotion data in blue-collar departments demonstrate that blacks are "in the pipeline." Table 3.22 details the experience of the yard for calendar year 1972.

As expected, the lower the job classification, the higher the proportion of the jobs held by blacks. Nonetheless, these data indicate that blacks are moving up in the system.

The number of women beginning blue-collar work in the shipyards has not been high. However, by 1974, women held jobs as operatives and craftsmen (although not as laborers). These women represent a breakthrough accomplished despite male resistance, and the Alabama Dry Dock experience has proved that women can be hired for blue-collar jobs and can be promoted in them.

In the past, blacks held some foremen's jobs in all-black units. However, not all predominantly black units had black foremen. It was initially charged that the company had practiced a general policy of placing white supervisors (in

TABLE 3.22

Promotions among Mechanics by Race, Alabama Dry Dock, 1972

Job Title	Total	White	Black	Percent Black	Percent White
First class mechanics	47	40	7	15.00	85.00
Second class mechanics	73	35	28	38.36	61.64
Third-class mechanics	11	6	5	45.45	54.55
All mechanics	121	81	40	33.06	66.94

Source: Document provided by Alabama Dry Dock Company.

the hourly permanent foreman categories) over some all-black units. However, by 1974 the yard had 25 black foremen in 12 departments, up from 13 black foremen in 3 departments in 1968.

The rate of black participation in the work force at the yard rose from 23 percent in 1970 to 31 percent in 1974. Moreover, the proportion of black craftsmen increased from 15 percent in 1970 to 22 percent in 1974. Thus, it can be concluded that participation by blacks in the work force at the yard was no longer a problem by 1974.

In blue-collar classifications, black mechanics were found in increasing percentages among promotions, new hires, and recalls. In addition, an increasing number of departments were promoting blacks to the permanent foreman level. In white-collar classifications, less numerical progress was made, but there were some changes from past patterns.

Summary and Conclusions

As noted earlier, shortly after the passage of the 1964 Civil Rights Act, both the union and the company began to show some uneasiness about the yard's past personnel practices. One manifestation of this was the establishment of a ten-member Bi-Racial Committee, half from management and half from the local union. All five of the management members come from the industrial relations department; the director of industrial relations is the chief of the management delegation. The union specifies that its two ranking officers—the president and executive secretary—are ex-officio members of the committee; the executive secretary is the ranking member of the union delegation. The remaining three members are black.

The management view of the Bi-Racial Committee is that it was established (at management's suggestion) to give blacks a voice which they had lacked in the past. The union view is that the committee was established (at union insistence) in order to facilitate harmony between the races.

The committee meets once a month for sessions which generally last over an hour. There is fairly common agreement among the parties that the committee has a small work load. Management contends that the largest amount of work for the committee concerns the dissatisfaction of employees with their current grade level. This is not properly an EEO matter, however, unless race or sex is a factor, which is rarely the case.

Union officials consider the small work load of the committee as an indication that there are no race problems at the yard. Outside civil rights observers and some black members of Local 18 consider the committee's small work load evidence of its lack of power. Some issues are resolved, but complaints just as regularly bypass the committee and are handled through the EEOC or the OCR in New Orleans.

The committee has apparently achieved the status which many observers attribute to the United Nations as well: Its successes are hard to win, but its promise is such that few are willing to recommend its abolition.

The company provides very little formal training for its potential or current employees. Some formal training courses do exist in crafts such as sheet metal, boilermaking, and the machine trades at the yard, but these must be taken on the individual's own time. The overwhelming portion of the training provided by the yard comes on the job, as was the case in the affected-class settlement (which specified that members of the affected class could receive 1,440 hours of training in the handyman program).

The NAACP and the Non-Partisan Voters League, both headquartered in Mobile, have been active in the cause of equal rights at the yard. They have primarily worked to help individual workers or job applicants in finding ways to file grievances with government agencies. These two organizations have publicized what they perceive to be the unfair practices of the yard, but overall, budgetary limitations have precluded their having much of a voice.

This evaluation of the efficacy of the federal government's enforcement in the area of employment discrimination at the Alabama Dry Dock and Shipbuilding Company is divided into three parts: the role of local labor-market pressures, the relationship between the affected-class settlement and the pattern of overall change, and the power of the federal government in the shipbuilding and ship repair industry, with special emphasis on its ability to impose sanctions under the authority of Executive Order 11246.

Any study of enforcement of antidiscrimination measures in employment requires an examination of local labor-market pressures. As noted above, ship repair involves unpleasant working conditions, with exposure to extremes of weather. Some slack existed in the local labor market (the unemployment rate in the Mobile SMSA fluctuated around 5 percent) during the time the details of the consent agreement were being negotiated. In addition, entrance standards were relaxed.

For example, the yard does not consider arrest records in applications for employment, and even convictions by themselves do not disqualify applicants. It could be argued that this practice allows a "second chance" for those who may have "gone wrong" earlier in life, but it is more probable that the yard followed this practice in the hope of attracting more workers.

It is our conclusion that the labor market was tighter for the Alabama Dry Dock Company than for most employers in the Mobile SMSA because of the unpleasant nature of ship repair work. Although this tightness may have influenced the increase in hiring of women for blue-collar occupations and blacks for higher job classifications, the yard may take credit for most of the upgrading of blacks and hiring of women which did occur.

Even a cursory examination of the results of the affected-class settlement and the change in the yard's work force between 1964 and 1974 (and particularly between 1970 and 1974) reveals that there is apparently no numerical relationship between the settlement and the changes in personnel practices. Some 62 persons have benefited directly from the affected-class settlement in an installation with some 950 black employees.

The government's enforcement efforts, however, have had a sizable influence on changes in the personnel operations of the yard. Changes in the work force since 1970 are evidence of this.

The federal government is heavily involved financially in shipbuilding and ship repair. The Alabama Dry Dock Company's major shipbuilding contracts in recent years have come from the navy, and the company has performed even more work, on a dollar-volume basis, on ship repair. This provides the federal government with considerable leverage. Some government contractors may be in a position to relinquish government business, but shipbuilders are not among them.

The other element influencing changes in the yard's employment practices has been the willingness of monitoring agencies, specifically the Department of Commerce, to impose sanctions. In addition, government administrators were able to rely on excellent staff work in the OCR.

The initial discussions with the Maritime Administration began in the spring of 1970 and continued until December 1972. The final resolution of the case, however, did not come until the union breach-of-contract suit was settled in December 1973 with the consent decree.

The federal government—with its imposition of sanctions—appears to have been the dominant force. The company needed government contracts and finally agreed to change the collective bargaining contract unilaterally. Although black workers in the yard had some assistance from the two local civil rights organizations, their cases were primarily handled by officials in the Maritime Administration and the EEOC.

Yard workers' only organized resistance to federal directives came through the union (which resisted to the last), even though such resistance cost it money and time, of which the union leadership was acutely conscious. Union intransigence reflected more than the state of race relations in Mobile, Alabama; it was designed to protect the unit seniority system and the employment rights of long-time employees in narrow craft divisions. The government had attacked the raison d'être of the union, which almost guaranteed its resistance.

TODD SHIPYARDS CORP. AND LOCKHEED SHIPBUILDING AND CONSTRUCTION IN SEATTLE

Seattle, Washington, has become known nationally as the city which best demonstrates the plight of exclusive dependence on the federal defense budget. The city experienced a huge unemployment rate between the late 1960s and

1974, resulting primarily from the decline in the aerospace industry (especially the Boeing operation in Seattle). Seattle's private shipbuilding and ship repair industry has also encountered problems.

The Actors and the Environment

The parties in the Seattle case were the managements of the two yards, a Metal Trades Council comprised of 11 unions, the Seattle Opportunities Industrialization Council, and the OCR.

The Seattle labor market suffered high unemployment throughout the period of this case. For example, early in 1971 the unemployment rate for King County (the Seattle SMSA) was 13 percent; the nonwhite unemployment rate was approximately 18 percent. Although the unemployment rate declined after 1971, the area continued to have an excess labor supply (see Table 3.23).

The 1970 minority population in King County was about 7 percent, split evenly between blacks and Spanish-surnamed Americans, Asians, and American Indians. Blacks constituted about 7 percent of Seattle's population; the other three groups constituted about 5.5 percent.

This case took place against a backdrop of the depressed Seattle economy and the erratic nature of shipbuilding and ship repair employment. Within 37 months—from April 1971 to May 1974—the total volume of employment doubled at the Todd yard, fell by nearly 90 percent, and moved back to about 80 percent of its peak employment (see Table 3.24). The Lockheed yard recorded a high of 4,400 employees in 1967, which subsequently fell to 1,500 by 1972 (see Table 3.25).

TABLE 3.23

Population and Employment in the Seattle SMSA 1970-73

	Years			
Series	1970	1971	1972	1973
Population	1,424,611	1,432,800	1,411,900	1,409,400
Civilian labor force	640,500	633,900	630,500	644,200
Employment	579,000	550,900	567,400	595,400
Unemployment rate (percent)	9.5	13.0	9.9	7.6

Source: Employment Security Department, State of Washington Annual Manpower Planning Report 1974, Seattle-Everett Washington Area.

TABLE 3.24

Total Employment at Todd-Seattle, October 1969–May 1974

Date	Total Employment
October 1969	3,421
April 1971	1,145
May 1972	2,222
April 1973	558
July 1973	250
May 1974	1,830

Source: Compliance Reviews, 1969–74.

TABLE 3.25

Employment Levels at Lockheed-Seattle, Selected Years, 1966–74

Year	Level of Employment
1966	4,276
1967	4,398
1969	3,782
1970	3,957
1971	2,367
1972	1,500
1973	1,737
January 1974	1,939

Source: Compliance Review Reports, various years, Office of Civil Rights, Maritime Administration.

With such economic conditions, OCR staff focused on retention of minorities and females. Management suggested that part of the problem stemmed from competition for skilled labor from construction and manufacturing industries, but with a loose local labor market this contention was difficult to accept. Construction wages do exceed those in shipyards, so in this respect the Seattle yards were no different from any other shipbuilder.

In addition to the different employment circumstances confronting the two Seattle yards as compared to those faced in the three previous cases, neither of the Seattle yards was subject to an affected-class settlement. It is therefore

TABLE 3.26

Composition of the Work Force by Sex, Race/Ethnic Group, and Occupational Category at the Todd–Seattle Shipyard, April 1971

Occupations	Male Employees						Female Employees					Total All Employees
	Total Males	Minority Groups				Total Females	Minority Groups				
		Black	Oriental	American Indian	Spanish American		Black	Oriental	American Indian	Spanish American	
Officials and managers	71	—	—	—	—	1	—	—	—	—	72
Professionals	66	1	—	—	—	2	—	—	—	—	68
Technicians	37	2	—	—	—	7	1	—	—	—	44
Sales workers	1	—	—	—	—	—	—	—	—	—	1
Office and clerical	26	4	2	—	—	40	1	—	—	—	66
Subtotal (white collar)	201	7	2	—	—	50	2	—	—	—	251
Craftsmen (skilled)	629	12	8	4	4	—	—	—	—	—	629
Operatives (semi-skilled)	157	6	2	4	6	—	—	—	—	—	157
Laborers (unskilled)	108	39	8	—	4	—	—	—	—	—	108
Service workers	0	—	—	—	—	—	—	—	—	—	0
Subtotal (blue collar)	894	57	18	8	14	—	—	—	—	—	894
Total	1,095	64	20	8	14	50	2	—	—	—	1,145

Source: EEO–1 report for 1971 from Todd Shipyard.

TABLE 3.27

Composition of the Work Force by Sex, Race/Ethnic Group, and Occupational Category at the Todd-Seattle Shipyard, May 1974

Occupations	Male Employees						Female Employees				
	Total Males	Minority Groups				Total Females	Minority Groups				Total All Employees
		Black	Oriental	American Indian	Spanish American		Black	Oriental	American Indian	Spanish American	
Officials and managers	71	1	1	1	–	1	–	–	–	–	72
Professionals	48	1	1	–	–	0	–	–	–	–	48
Technicians	59	3	–	–	–	11	2	–	–	–	70
Sales workers	1	–	–	–	–	0	–	–	–	–	1
Office and clerical	16	1	–	–	–	34	1	–	–	–	50
Subtotal (white collar)	195	6	2	1	0	46	3	0	0	0	241
Craftsmen (skilled)	1,444	47	27	23	27	9	–	–	–	–	1,453
Operatives (semi-skilled)	39	1	0	1	1	0	–	–	–	–	39
Laborers (unskilled)	82	52	5	1	4	8	2	–	–	–	90
Service workers	7	3	0	0	0	0	–	–	–	–	7
Subtotal (blue collar)	1,572	103	32	25	32	17	2	0	0	0	1,589
Total	1,767	109	34	26	32	63	5	0	0	0	1,830

Source: EEO-1 report for 1974 from Todd Shipyard.

instructive to examine the impact of continuing surveillance by the equal opportunity specialist in the Seattle branch of the OCR under these different circumstances.

This can be done by combining statistical materials with compliance review reports. Responses to compliance reviews, often in the form of amended affirmative action plans, constitute another example of out-of-court settlements. If no case can be made for an affected-class settlement, the OCR has to depend on regular compliance reviews to produce change. However, at the Lockheed yard, the equal opportunity specialist apparently chose not to press for an affected-class settlement, even though a case could have been made for one.

Continuing Surveillance at the Todd Yard

As shown in Tables 3.26 and 3.27, from April 1971 to May 1974, total employment at the Todd yard increased from 1,145 to 1,830; during that period, employment had risen to 2,222 in May 1972 and fallen to 250 in July 1973.

Total employment and percent of employment are shown for females in Table 3.28. Between April 1971 and May 1974, employment for minorities at Todd increased from approximately 9 percent to slightly over 11 percent (see Table 3.29). Hence, there has been no argument about Todd's meeting the standard OFCC benchmark of employment for minorities commensurate with their percentage in the local labor market, which in the Seattle SMSA is slightly over 7 percent.

The number of minority craftsmen jumped from 28 to 124 as the total number of craftsmen increased from 629 to 1,453. This represented a shift from 4.4 percent to 8 percent. Clerical jobs fell from 66 percent to 50 percent during a tremendous expansion in employment, resulting in a disproportionate decline in minority clerical workers from seven to two positions. In the top three classifications—officials and managers, professionals, and technicians—the percentage of minorities increased from 2.2 percent to 5.3 percent (an absolute increase from four positions to ten positions).

In sum, there was a small increase in the overall participation of minorities, a near doubling of their craft positions, a loss of five clerical jobs, and an increase from four to ten jobs in the top three occupational categories.

Even in a period of decline, a firm may hire new employees. Between October 1969 and April 1971, employment at the yard decreased from 3,421 to 1,145, but there were 471 new hires in nine craft and five laborer classifications between March 1970 and March 1971. About one-fourth (24 percent) of these hires were minorities, but some 94 percent of this group were in semiskilled or unskilled categories.

TABLE 3.28

Todd–Seattle 1971–74 Comparisons: Females to Total

Year	Total Employment	Total Female Employment	Percent Female	Craft			Clerical			Officers & Managers, Professionals, and Technicians		
				Female	Total	Percent Female	Female	Total	Percent Female	Female	Total	Percent Female
1971	1,145	50	4.36	0	629		40	66	61	10	184	5.0
1974	1,830	63	3.44	9	1,453	.01	34	50	68	12	190	6.0

Source: EEO–1 forms for 1971 and 1974.

TABLE 3.29

Todd–Seattle 1971–74 Comparisons: Minorities to Total

Year	Total Employment	Total Minority Employment	Percent Minority	Craft			Clerical			Officers & Managers, Professionals, and Technicians		
				Minority	Total	Percent Minority	Minority	Total	Percent Minority	Minority	Total	Percent Minority
1971	1,145	108	9.42	28	629	4.4	7	66	10.6	4	184	2.2
1974	1,830	206	11.26	124	1,453	8.0	2	50	4.0	10	190	5.3

Source: EEO–1 forms for 1971 and 1974.

115

Compliance reviews were conducted by an equal opportunity specialist stationed in Seattle. The specialist found that the yard was not in compliance from October 1969 through March 1971, but this did not lead to sanctions of any kind. Work began declining in early 1970, and after the 1969 review found the yard to be in a state of noncompliance, a revised affirmative action plan was required. By the time this document was accepted by the Maritime Administration on June 22, 1970, employment at the yard was decreasing rapidly, with no apparent end in sight.

The equal opportunity specialist and his supervisor in the San Francisco regional office believed it would be unrealistic to expect the yard to fulfill its goals and timetables even in spite of its new hires. By 1973 the San Francisco regional office ceased considering Todd's EEO stance because of the continuing deteriorating economic situation in Seattle. Employment had increased, however, to roughly 1,800 by the time the equal opportunity specialist conducted another review in May 1974.

This layoff/recall activity had important implications for minority employment. The Todd yard's personnel policy gave employees callback rights if they had worked for 260 consecutive days in the three years immediately prior to layoff. The erratic nature of Todd's business therefore precluded the earning of recall rights by many employees.

Employees could have the equivalent of recall rights, however, by virtue of union membership. The collective bargaining agreement contained a clause requiring the yard to give the 11 unions 48 hours to find qualified applicants to fill each opening. This procedure was so integral to the personnel process that portions of it appear in the affirmative action plan. (Indeed, the revised affirmative action plan submitted in May 1973 reads as if it could have been written by union officials.) This tight control by the unions put them in a position to influence the implementation of the aims spelled out in Todd's affirmative action plan.

Both the recall procedure and the union referral procedure could have perpetuated past discriminatory practices in regard to race and sex. In order to discover why this did not happen, the compliance review of May 1974 must be examined.

By May 1974 the minority participation rate had risen about 1.8 percentage points, but the rate for females had fallen by about 1 percentage point. The equal opportunity specialist reasoned that the yard deserved to be held in compliance, though, because it had placed females and minorities into nontraditional jobs and was making good-faith efforts to implement its affirmative action plan. The company had some problems, but the specialist believed that its recent record indicated a willingness—especially considering the current economic context—to take affirmative action.

Continuing Surveillance at the Lockheed Yard

From March 1970 to March 1974, the overall level of employment at Lockheed declined from a high of roughly 4,000 to a low of 1,500 and then increased to 2,100 (see Table 3.30). The participation rate for minorities fluctuated from a low of around 11 percent to a high of 15 percent. Minorities consistently held about 14 percent of the represented craft classifications, which included all blue-collar jobs; by 1974, minorities held 17 percent of these jobs (see Table 3.31).

TABLE 3.30

Minority Participation Rates, Lockheed-Seattle, March 1970–March 1974

Year	Number of Employees	Black	Spanish-surnamed Americans	Others	Total Minorities	Percent
March 1970	3,957	354	43	95	492	12.4
May 1971	2,367	254	27	55	336	14.1
May 1972	1,500	123	19	32	174	11.6
May 1973	1,737	128	23	59	210	12.1
March 1974	2,161	211	34	86	331	15.3

Source: Compliance Review Report, 1974.

TABLE 3.31

Represented Craft Employees, Minorities and Total, Lockheed-Seattle, March 1970–March 1974

Year	Number of Employees	Black	Spanish-surnamed Americans	Others	Total Minorities	Percent
March 1970	3,251	339	39	75	453	13.9
May 1971	1,965	248	24	46	318	16.2
May 1972	1,096	120	15	20	155	14.1
May 1973	1,380	124	20	50	194	14.1
March 1974	1,819	206	29	76	311	17.1

Source: Compliance Review Report, 1974.

TABLE 3.32

Hourly Nonrepresented Employees, Lockheed–Seattle, March 1970–1974

Year	Number of Employees	Blacks	Spanish-surnamed Americans	Others	Total Minorities	Percent
March 1970	356	11	2	16	29	8.1
May 1971	174	4	1	6	11	6.3
May 1972	171	3	2	8	12	7.0
May 1973	154	3	2	5	10	6.5
March 1974	148	5	2	7	14	9.5

Source: Compliance Review Report, 1974.

TABLE 3.33

Salaried Nonrepresented Employees, Lockheed–Seattle, March 1970–March 1974

Year	Number of Employees	Blacks	Spanish-surnamed Americans	Others	Total Minorities	Percent
March 1970	350	4	2	4	10	2.8
May 1971	228	2	2	3	7	3.1
May 1972	233	1	2	4	7	3.0
May 1973	203	1	1	4	6	3.0
March 1974	194	—	3	3	6	3.1

Source: Compliance Review Report, 1974.

Throughout this four-year period, minorities represented 6 to 9 percent of the white-collar workers paid on an hourly basis and not represented by a union (see Table 3.32). Minorities have never represented more than ten jobs in the top three classifications (salaried nonrepresented jobs), or about 3 percent of these white-collar positions (see Table 3.33).

The equal opportunity specialist in Seattle has been understandably concerned about the retention of minority and female workers throughout this period of economic distress. The specialist and company officials reached an understanding that when business improved, goals and timetables would be revised to concentrate on those areas where the yard was deficient.

Since our data encompass the period from March 1970 to March 1974, it is appropriate to compare the compliance reviews conducted in May 1969 and January 1974. (The completion of the latter was delayed because of OCR dissatisfaction leading to some revisions in Lockheed's affirmative action plan.)

The conclusion of the 1969 review was that the contractor "was in a state of noncompliance, but contract awardable." This curious finding meant that the contractor had serious EEO deficiencies but that agreement had been reached on what remedies were necessary and that the OCR had accepted the agreement as having been struck in good faith. Most of the deficiencies were those common in industry: Minorities and women held few of the better-paying, higher-skilled jobs.

The equal opportunity specialist was also concerned, however, about the existence of an affected class. It is of interest because the OCR attempted to eliminate this violation by constant surveillance instead of implementing the affected-class remedy sought elsewhere. The reasons for this choice are unclear, but the deteriorating economic situation in Seattle and the concentration of the OCR's resources in the East and on the Gulf Coast in seeking affected-class settlements were probably influential.

The affected class was composed of blacks who worked as scalers belonging to a separate laborers' union, one of the 11 unions comprising the Metal Trades Council. The scaler's job is hard, dirty, and of low status. Through a combination of employee preference and company policies, blacks represented over 90 percent of the scalers' unit by the time of the 1969 compliance review. Perpetuating these circumstances were the transfer provisions in the company's agreement with the Metal Trades Council and the small wage differentials between scaling and other jobs.

The collective bargaining agreement specified that an employee gained seniority in a line of progression covered by a constituent union in the Metal Trades Council. Members of one union could work in another line and hold membership in two locals, but there was no provision for carry-forward seniority. This acts as a disincentive to mobility, a disincentive augmented by the small economic gains to be made by transferring. For instance, the hourly wage difference between the scaler's and journeyman's pay was $.13 in 1969 and $.14 in 1974. This kind of wage leveling has had a similar disincentive effect in other yards.

The OCR asked Lockheed to pursue imaginative solutions to this problem. Since the volume of orders declined before any substantive results could be attained, the OCR turned its attention to retention. The company continued to be classified as "contract awardable," even though it fared poorly compared to the goals of its affirmative action plan.

TABLE 3.34

Minority Participation in Selected Crafts, Lockheed–Seattle, 1972–74

	Crafts		
	Pipefitters	Sheet metal	Welders
1972			
Total	67	52	225
Minority	5	1	33
Percent	7.5	1.9	14.7
1973			
Total	122	94	371
Minority	10	5	68
Percent	8.2	5.3	18.3
1974			
Total	205	134	454
Minority	18	10	96
Percent	8.8	7.5	21.1

Note: For the second consecutive year an increase is noted in three of the major craft areas. Not indicated in the above figures is the employment of the first female in the machinist trade in the tool room/repair classification.

Source: Compliance Review Report, 1974.

In the 1974 compliance review, the OCR discerned no change in the collective-bargaining agreement but held that none of the unions applied the agreement differently to minorities or women than to white males; thus, it was concluded that the company could not be faulted for its retention efforts (see Tables 3.31–3.33).

In addition, the color distribution in the scalers' unit changed somewhat by its inclusion of more nonminorities. Movement by blacks out of the unit has been minimal, and the increases in minority membership in other unions have benefited young nonwhites.

Many problems remain at Lockheed, but the number of blue-collar units with few minorities has been reduced. Progress has been understandably slow, given the economic situation. The upswing in business activity in 1974 was, fortunately, accompanied by some progress for equal opportunity at Lockheed (see Table 3.34 in particular).

Remaining Issues at Todd and Lockheed

A discussion of three other issues will complete the analysis of the Seattle experience: the status of women, the Seattle Opportunities Industrialization Council, and the Local 86 case.[21]

The primary issue with respect to women (although this has hardly been confined to shipyards) has been their employment in nontraditional jobs. Women have participated in blue-collar work since the impetus of the Civil Rights Act of 1964 and Executive Order 11375, but such employment has often been on a token basis. The Seattle yards are such an example.

At Todd, when the work force increased by 62 percent, the employment of women increased from 50 positions to only 63 positions, so their participation rate actually declined from 4.4 percent to 3.4 percent (see Tables 3.26 and 3.27). The number of women in the top three classifications rose from 10 to 12, but most of these were technicians, not managers, officials, or professionals. At the same time, however, nine nonminority women were hired for craft jobs. In sum, Todd experienced an overall decline, with a breakthrough only in craft jobs. The percentage of women employed at Lockheed was low but remained steady between 1970 and 1974 (see Table 3.35).

However, in 1974, both companies and the Metal Trades Council were attempting, albeit belatedly, to hire women for the skilled crafts. Progress has

TABLE 3.35

Female Employees: Total and Minority, Lockheed-Seattle, March 1970–March 1974

Year	Number of Employees	Caucasian	Blacks	Spanish-surnamed Americans	Others	Percent of Work Force	Percent Minorities
March 1970	153	140	3	2	8	3.8	2.0
May 1971	82	77	2	0	3	3.4	6.1
May 1972	73	68	1	0	4	4.8	6.8
May 1973	63	58	2	1	2	3.6	7.9
March 1974	77	66	5	1	5	3.6	14.3

Source: Compliance Review Report, 1974.

been minimal, but a breakthrough has occurred. As employment increases in the Seattle yards, more progress can be expected.

The Seattle Opportunities Industrialization Council (SOIC) has been a successful contractor in training aspiring shipbuilders as welders for Lockheed. The company contracted with the SOIC twice for 60 welders to be trained; the contract provided for SOIC to be paid more the longer its placements remain with the shipyard. By the expiration of the second contract, SOIC had placed over 100 welders at the facility, more then 20 percent of whom were minorities; six were women.

The celebrated Ironworkers Local 86 case had an upsetting effect on Todd and Lockheed, because that part of the remedy giving black journeymen preferential referral treatment to construction jobs caused the yard to lose black employees to the construction industry.

Summary

The distinguishing characteristics of the Todd and Lockheed cases were the lack of drama and the effect of adverse economic conditions. The economic situation was the main determinant of the outcome in each case. Economic conditions meant that the companies were trying to maintain their levels of employment, the unions were struggling to protect their members, and the OCR was primarily concerned with retention of women and minorities.

The absence of an affected-class settlement at Lockheed was attributable to the demands made on the OCR's resources by the affected-class settlements in the East and on the Gulf Coast. Economic conditions alone, however, were sufficient to justify the decision not to intervene; a settlement could not have produced much change. The OCR decided to continue its strategy of continuing surveillance instead.

The overall participation rate by minorities at the yards has not been a problem. Most of the areas examined by the equal opportunity specialist concerned imbalances of minorities and females by department; some improvement was achieved in this area in both yards.

Women were eventually placed in nontraditional jobs, but only on a token basis. Minorities increased their participation in the crafts also; that increase was facilitated by a training agreement between the yards and the Metal Trades Council. Although some nonwhites were added to the scalers unit, the entire affected-class problem at Lockheed remains to be settled.

In the face of declining employment, it is no surprise that little could be done for equal employment opportunity. The most the OCR could have done, besides its emphasis on retention, was to prepare for the future. Except for prescribing the standard remedies for an affected class, it has done so.

POSTSCRIPT

These case studies relied on data sources from reports filed no later than 1973 or 1974. The following five tables provide an update for 1974 and 1977 for each yard. The format features a display of female and minority-group participation and occupational position.

Between these two recent years there has been a general upward movement in minority-group participation in four of the five yards. There have been some small improvements in occupational standing for minority groups also. The most important recent change has been in the increasing participation of women in blue-collar craft positions. It is likely that this experience in the nation's shipyards will be seen as a pacesetter for the entry of women in a wider range of craft, blue-collar occupations throughout the economy.

TABLE 3.36

Employees by Race, Sex, and Major Job Category, 1974 and 1977, Lockheed Shipbuilding and Construction, Seattle

	Total Work Force				Total Minorities				Black		Native American		Hispanic		Asian Pacific	
	Total		Female		Total		Female									
Year	No.	%	No.	%	No.	%	No.	%	No.	%	No.	%	No.	%	No.	%
Total work force																
1974	1,918	100.0	65	3.3	257	13.3	4	.2	156	8.1	23	1.1	28	1.4	50	2.6
1977	2,935	100.0	177	6.0	475	16.1	45	1.5	257	8.7	24	.8	47	1.6	147	5.0
Officials and managers																
1974	116	100.0	—	—	3	2.5	—	—	1	.8	—	—	—	—	2	1.7
1977	126	100.0	2	1.5	4	3.1	—	—	2	1.5	2	1.5	—	—	—	—
Professionals																
1974	96	100.0	—	—	2	2.0	—	—	—	—	—	—	1	1.0	1	1.0
1977	136	100.0	4	2.9	8	5.8	—	—	2	1.4	2	1.4	2	1.4	2	1.4

Technicians															
1974	51	100.0	7	13.7	5	9.8	1	1.9	3	5.8	1	1.9	1	1.9	–	–
1977	96	100.0	7	7.2	6	6.2	2	2.0	2	2.0	1	1.0	2	2.0	1	1.0
Clerical															
1974	57	100.0	44	77.1	5	8.7	3	5.2	1	1.7	1	1.7	–	–	3	5.2
1977	88	100.0	68	77.2	11	12.5	9	10.2	5	5.6	–	–	1	1.1	5	5.6
Crafts (skilled)															
1974	1,359	100.0	14	1.0	154	11.3	–	–	70	5.1	19	1.3	24	1.7	41	3.0
1977	2,075	100.0	50	2.4	307	14.7	10	.4	127	6.1	11	.5	39	1.8	130	6.2
Operatives (semiskilled)															
1974	132	100.0	–	–	8	6.0	–	–	3	2.2	1	.7	2	1.5	2	1.5
1977	222	100.0	3	1.3	16	7.2	–	–	4	1.8	6	2.7	1	.4	5	2.2
Laborers (unskilled)															
1974	92	100.0	–	–	80	86.9	–	–	78	84.7	1	1.0	–	–	1	1.0
1977	176	100.0	42	23.8	123	69.8	24	13.6	115	65.3	2	1.1	2	1.1	4	2.2
Service workers															
1974	15	100.0	–	–	–	–	–	–	–	–	–	–	–	–	–	–
1977	16	100.0	1	6.2	–	–	–	–	–	–	–	–	–	–	–	–

Source: EEO–1 Report data filed with OCR, Maritime Administration. These reports are filed each January.

TABLE 3.37

Employees by Race, Sex, and Major Job Category, 1974 and 1977, Newport News Shipbuilding and Dry Dock Co.

| | Total Work Force | | | | Total Minorities | | | | Black | | Native American | | Hispanic | | Asian Pacific | |
| | Total | | Female | | Total | | Female | | | | | | | | | |
Year	No.	%	No.	%	No.	%	No.	%	No.	%	No.	%	No.	%	No.	%
Total work force																
1974	23,993	100.0	1,775	7.3	8,003	33.3	422	1.7	8,003	33.3	—	—	—	—	—	—
1977	22,956	100.0	1,731	7.5	8,298	36.1	543	2.3	8,298	36.1	—	—	—	—	—	—
Officials and managers																
1974	3,051	100.0	21	.6	270	8.8	—	—	270	8.8	—	—	—	—	—	—
1977	2,511	100.0	17	.6	288	11.4	—	—	288	11.4	—	—	—	—	—	—
Professionals																
1974	3,408	100.0	97	2.8	159	4.6	16	.4	159	4.6	—	—	—	—	—	—
1977	2,512	100.0	65	2.5	123	4.8	11	.4	123	4.8	—	—	—	—	—	—

	Total																			
Technicians																				
1974	1,473	100.0	58	3.9	265	17.9	10	.6	265	17.9	—	—	—	—	—	—	—	—	—	—
1977	1,066	100.0	42	3.9	187	17.5	8	.7	187	17.5	—	—	—	—	—	—	—	—	—	—
Clerical																				
1974	2,346	100.0	1,026	43.7	768	32.7	273	11.6	768	32.7	—	—	—	—	—	—	—	—	—	—
1977	1,495	100.0	765	51.1	498	33.3	206	13.7	498	33.3	—	—	—	—	—	—	—	—	—	—
Crafts (skilled)																				
1974	8,011	100.0	115	1.4	3,488	43.5	18	.2	3,488	43.5	—	—	—	—	—	—	—	—	—	—
1977	9,639	100.0	220	2.2	4,416	45.8	75	.7	4,416	45.8	—	—	—	—	—	—	—	—	—	—
Operatives (semiskilled)																				
1974	2,295	100.0	29	1.2	1,358	59.1	7	.3	1,358	59.1	—	—	—	—	—	—	—	—	—	—
1977	2,072	100.0	183	8.8	1,101	53.1	58	2.7	1,101	53.1	—	—	—	—	—	—	—	—	—	—
Laborers (unskilled)																				
1974	2,971	100.0	387	13.0	1,471	49.5	87	2.9	1,471	49.5	—	—	—	—	—	—	—	—	—	—
1977	3,256	100.0	387	11.8	1,508	46.3	172	5.2	1,508	46.3	—	—	—	—	—	—	—	—	—	—
Service workers																				
1974	437	100.0	42	9.6	224	51.2	11	2.5	224	51.2	—	—	—	—	—	—	—	—	—	—
1977	404	100.0	52	12.8	177	43.8	13	3.2	177	43.8	—	—	—	—	—	—	—	—	—	—

Source: EEO-1 Report data filed with OCR, Maritime Administration.

TABLE 3.38

Employees by Race, Sex, and Major Job Category, 1974 and 1977, Ingalls Shipbuilding Division, Litton Industries

Year	Total Work Force				Total Minorities				Black		Native American		Hispanic		Asian Pacific	
	Total		Female		Total		Female									
	No.	%	No.	%	No.	%	No.	%	No.	%	No.	%	No.	%	No.	%
Total work force																
1974	18,902	100.0	2,289	12.1	4,598	24.3	903	4.7	4,471	23.6	120	.6	—	—	7	—
1977	24,600	100.0	3,760	15.2	7,320	29.7	1,664	6.7	7,207	29.2	113	.4	—	—	—	—
Officials and managers																
1974	1,923	100.0	42	2.1	128	6.6	8	.4	121	6.2	7	.3	—	—	—	—
1977	2,429	100.0	70	2.8	308	12.6	16	.6	306	12.5	2	.1	—	—	—	—
Professionals																
1974	2,494	100.0	146	5.8	164	6.5	27	1.0	156	6.2	5	.2	—	—	3	.1
1977	1,480	100.0	119	8.0	102	6.8	22	1.4	95	6.4	7	.4	—	—	—	—

Technicians															
1974	1,220	100.0	142	11.6	144	11.8	29	2.3	140	11.4	4	.3	—	—	—
1977	2,045	100.0	377	18.4	303	14.8	85	4.1	297	14.5	6	.2	—	—	—
Clerical															
1974	1,043	100.0	949	90.9	233	22.3	204	19.5	229	21.9	3	.2	—	1	—
1977	1,271	100.0	1,066	83.8	365	28.7	296	23.2	358	28.1	7	.5	—	—	—
Crafts (skilled)															
1974	5,976	100.0	116	1.9	1,235	20.6	77	1.2	1,212	20.2	20	.3	—	3	—
1977	8,158	100.0	450	5.5	2,225	27.2	291	3.5	2,201	26.9	24	.2	—	—	—
Operatives (semiskilled)															
1974	5,412	100.0	657	12.1	2,244	41.4	411	7.5	2,167	40.0	77	1.4	—	—	—
1977	8,147	100.0	1,217	14.9	3,298	40.4	587	7.2	3,240	39.7	58	.7	—	—	—
Laborers (unskilled)															
1974	572	100.0	145	25.3	371	64.8	108	18.8	368	64.3	3	.5	—	—	—
1977	943	100.0	447	47.4	689	73.0	360	38.1	680	72.1	9	.9	—	—	—
Service workers															
1974	262	100.0	92	35.1	79	30.1	39	14.8	78	29.7	1	.3	—	—	—
1977	127	100.0	14	11.0	30	23.6	7	5.5	30	23.6	—	—	—	—	—

Source: EEO–1 Report data filed with OCR, Maritime Administration.

TABLE 3.39

Employees by Race, Sex, and Major Job Category, 1974 and 1977, Alabama Dry Dock and Shipbuilding Co.

Year	Total Work Force				Total Minorities											
	Total		Female		Total		Female		Black		Native American		Hispanic		Asian Pacific	
	No.	%	No.	%	No.	%	No.	%	No.	%	No.	%	No.	%	No.	%
Total work force																
1974	2,934	100.0	106	3.6	940	32.0	23	.7	940	32.0	—	—	—	—	—	—
1977	3,437	100.0	182	5.2	1,297	37.7	74	2.1	1,287	37.4	—	—	6	.1	4	.1
Officials and managers																
1974	75	100.0	2	2.6	1	1.3	—	—	1	1.3	—	—	—	—	—	—
1977	72	100.0	3	4.1	4	5.5	—	—	4	5.5	—	—	—	—	—	—
Professionals																
1974	76	100.0	8	10.5	4	5.2	—	—	4	5.2	—	—	—	—	—	—
1977	82	100.0	9	10.9	4	4.8	—	—	4	4.8	—	—	—	—	—	—

130

Category / Year	Total	%	No.	%	No.	%	No.	%	No.	%	No.	%	No.	%	No.	%	No.
Technicians																	
1974	41	100.0	6	14.6	4	9.7	1	2.4	4	9.7	—	—	—	—	—	—	—
1977	38	100.0	10	26.3	3	7.8	2	5.2	3	7.8	—	—	—	—	—	—	—
Clerical																	
1974	120	100.0	69	57.5	14	11.6	9	7.5	14	11.6	—	—	—	—	—	—	—
1977	108	100.0	71	65.7	16	14.8	8	7.4	16	14.8	—	—	—	—	—	—	—
Crafts (skilled)																	
1974	1,747	100.0	11	.6	390	22.3	5	.2	390	22.3	—	—	—	—	5	—	—
1977	2,224	100.0	72	3.2	724	32.5	49	2.2	717	32.2	—	.2	—	.2	2	2	—
Operatives (semiskilled)																	
1974	632	100.0	4	.6	341	53.9	2	.3	341	53.9	—	—	—	—	1	—	—
1977	634	100.0	8	1.2	329	51.8	7	1.1	326	51.4	—	.1	—	.1	2	2	.3
Laborers (unskilled)																	
1974	200	100.0	—	—	166	83.0	—	—	166	83.0	—	—	—	—	—	—	—
1977	225	100.0	3	1.3	193	85.7	3	1.3	193	85.7	—	—	—	—	—	—	—
Service workers																	
1974	42	100.0	6	14.2	20	47.6	6	14.2	20	47.6	—	—	—	—	—	—	—
1977	53	100.0	6	11.3	24	45.2	5	9.4	24	45.2	—	—	—	—	—	—	—

Source: EEO-1 Report data filed with OCR, Maritime Administration.

TABLE 3.40

Employees by Race, Sex, and Major Job Category, 1974 and 1977, Todd Shipyards Corp., Seattle

Year	Total Work Force				Total Minorities											
	Total		Female		Total		Female		Black		Native American		Hispanic		Asian Pacific	
	No.	%	No.	%	No.	%	No.	%	No.	%	No.	%	No.	%	No.	%
Total work force																
1974	1,162	100.0	46	3.9	142	12.2	2	.1	91	7.8	17	1.4	11	.9	23	1.9
1977	1,074	100.0	69	6.4	121	11.2	11	1.0	61	5.6	15	1.3	19	1.7	26	2.4
Officials and managers																
1974	72	100.0	1	1.3	3	4.1	–	–	1	1.3	1	1.3	–	–	1	1.3
1977	74	100.0	2	2.7	4	5.4	–	–	2	2.7	1	1.3	–	–	1	1.3
Professionals																
1974	37	100.0	–	–	–	–	–	–	–	–	–	–	–	–	–	–
1977	55	100.0	3	5.4	2	3.6	–	–	1	1.8	–	–	–	–	1	1.8

	Total															
	N	%	N	%	N	%	N	%	N	%	N	%	N	%	N	%
Technicians																
1974	53	100.0	8	15.0	3	5.6	1	1.8	3	5.6	—	—	—	—	—	—
1977	43	100.0	9	20.9	4	9.3	1	2.3	4	9.3	—	—	—	—	—	—
Clerical																
1974	44	100.0	29	65.9	2	4.5	—	—	1	2.2	—	—	—	—	1	2.2
1977	53	100.0	46	86.7	9	16.9	8	15.0	3	5.6	—	—	3	5.6	3	5.6
Crafts (skilled)																
1974	868	100.0	3	.3	70	8.0	1	.1	29	3.3	15	1.7	11	1.2	15	1.7
1977	755	100.0	3	.3	56	7.4	—	—	15	1.9	13	1.7	10	1.3	18	2.3
Operatives (semiskilled)																
1974	40	100.0	—	—	31	77.5	—	—	28	70.0	—	—	—	—	3	7.5
1977	38	100.0	1	2.6	2	5.2	—	—	—	—	—	—	1	2.6	1	2.6
Laborers (unskilled)																
1974	40	100.0	4	10.0	30	75.0	—	—	26	65.0	1	2.5	—	—	3	7.5
1977	53	100.0	4	7.5	42	79.2	1	1.8	35	66.0	1	1.8	4	7.5	2	3.7
Service workers																
1974	7	100.0	1	14.2	3	42.8	—	—	3	42.8	—	—	—	—	—	—
1977	3	100.0	1	33.3	2	66.6	1	33.3	1	33.3	—	—	1	33.3	—	—

Source: EEO-1 Report data filed with OCR, Maritime Administration.

133

CONCLUSIONS

This study of employment patterns in the shipbuilding and ship repair industry is primarily an evaluation of the effectiveness of the enforcement mechanisms used by the OCR under the aegis of the Office of Federal Contract Compliance in the Department of Labor.

A major conclusion of this study is that the OCR has been most effective in those yards where it has negotiated an affected-class settlement; however, there is no apparent numerical connection between these settlements and the achievement of compliance.

Participating in these negotiations and implementing the settlements produced a need to revamp entire personnel systems. This revamping of personnel systems in line with the Civil Rights Act of 1964 and the requirements of government contracts is the change that produced compliance. Many factors contributed to successful compliance, but the moving force was the resolution of the Maritime Administration that the law would be enforced.

The civil rights revolution has produced numerous changes in industrial relations practices. The shipbuilding and ship repair industry has been the setting for many of these changes; hence this study encountered several issues common to other industries, including: the quality of the civil rights enforcement efforts; the impact of local labor-market pressures; the changing role of corporate personnel offices; the role of organized labor; the contribution of outreach and agencies employing outreach efforts; the placement of women in nontraditional jobs; the use of shipyards as training institutions and of benchmarks drawn from census data; and the future of affected-class settlements.

The Efficacy of the Office of Civil Rights

As noted previously, one of the most important factors responsible for success in these cases was the staff work and supervision of the OCR in Washington, D.C., which studies the latest developments in Title VII law and the consent decrees achieved by the EEOC and other contract compliance agencies. As Title VII settlements began to include back-pay awards and the restructuring of seniority systems, the OCR adopted these elements as part of its package to be used in negotiations.

For example, the early affected-class settlements did not include the demand for back pay for members of the affected class. Once OCR leadership became convinced that back pay could be won in the courts under Title VII, however, that demand was added to the negotiating package.

Further, in the Newport News affected-class settlement, the members of the class were allowed to transfer to new departments, but they had no carry-forward seniority. Later, when the issue of carry-forward seniority was settled in the courts, the new affected-class settlements contained that arrangement for members of the affected class.

These two examples suggest that industries which "put their houses in order" at a late date may have to accept broader packages, a point which has not been lost on personnel officials in shipbuilding and ship repair.

In addition to using compliance reviews to effect appropriate action to accompany the promises of affirmative action plans, the OCR has worked out an effective informal complaint procedure. Aggrieved minorities and women know that their complaints will be received with sympathy in the regional offices of the Maritime Administration. Sometimes complaints are transmitted by letter or telephone; sometimes they are forwarded "secondhand" through a "resident radical." (Each yard has a person or organization familiar with its personnel operation who is well acquainted with the OCR regional staff. Sometimes the transmitting agent is an employee of the yard, but not always.)

Thus individual charges are brought informally to the attention of equal opportunity specialists in the regional OCR offices, where they are reviewed to determine "probable cause." The first effort toward resolution attempts to obtain more information from the company and union(s) about the charge. This is done primarily by telephone.

If the equal opportunity specialist determines that there is no basis for the charge, the case is dismissed. Occasionally grievances are resolved over the telephone. More often, the equal opportunity specialist collects and consolidates various charges, gaining increasing amounts of information about them and holding them until the next on-site review.

Toward the end of the on-site review, the equal opportunity specialist discusses each charge face-to-face with the "respondent." The usual procedure is to obtain an agreement, which is transmitted in the compliance review report to the senior compliance officer in Washington, D.C., for approval. Many individual cases are resolved in this way, albeit with varying amounts of negotiation.

The informal charges may point to a practice which needs to be altered (rather than an individual case of mistreatment to be corrected). The settlement procedure has the advantage of speed compared to the delay common with the slow-moving machinery of the EEOC. However, personnel officials are unlikely to grant back pay in such settlements. Some yards have agreed to make double promotions in lieu of back pay, though, so this procedure represents an expeditious method of resolving conflicts.

Still, the procedure has its detractors. Many union officials prefer to file a grievance complaint under the collective bargaining contract instead (the use of one avenue does not preclude the use of another, however). In addition, some interviewees at the yards felt that EEOC staff might be more willing than OCR staff to push for back pay.

The procedure also entails the potential hazard that the OCR staff and the personnel officers or union officials involved may develop a personal relationship that encourages the swapping of grievances. However, such a hazard also occurs under collective bargaining agreements. Overall, the procedure is worthy of use, despite its drawbacks.

Bargaining for affected-class settlements is a grueling exercise requiring considerable expertise. The OCR has access to the necessary legal staff. The crucial ingredient to the success of this approach, however, is support from the top. This has been forthcoming from the Maritime Administrator—who was determined to enforce the executive order—and the staff of the OCR, backed by the administrator's authority.

The Impact of Local Labor-Market Conditions

One of the problems in research on the impact of civil rights enforcement efforts in employment has been the difficulty of untangling the effect of local labor-market conditions from other factors involved. For instance, it might be argued that tight labor-market conditions produce higher participation rates for women and minorities. Likewise, it might be contended that the same conditions produce higher relative occupational standing for those two groups.

However, as demonstrated in the two-volume study *Employment of Southern Blacks*, this is a gross oversimplification (if not actually incorrect).[22] The conclusion of that study was that tight labor-market conditions could provide a setting for changing the level of participation and relative occupational standing but that tight labor markets by themselves could not produce higher participation rates.

The generally tight labor markets in Newport News and at the two Gulf Coast yards constituted a favorable setting, especially considering the growing demand for employees at these yards. Because of its tradition, the Newport News yard had always had a high participation rate by blacks. However, participation rates for blacks at the Gulf Coast yards ceased to be a problem only after enforcement efforts under the authority of Title VII and the executive order. The yards did need employees, and blacks were available, so labor-market tightness can be given some credit for rising participation rates, but their timing was very closely associated with the period after the Civil Rights Act of 1964.

The improvement in occupational standing by blacks and the breakthrough of women into nontraditional jobs must be attributed to the change in focus of the yard personnel systems. This change was brought about by enforcement efforts of the federal government.

The Seattle yards experienced a wholly different set of economic conditions. Their volume of business fell drastically in what was already a slack labor market. No favorable setting existed for improving the status of minorities and women. Even though some changes did occur in upgrading and the placement of women in nontraditional jobs, our conclusion is that labor-market tightness is a necessary but insufficient condition to achieve improvement in participation rates.

The Changing Role of Corporate Personnel Offices

The major change in corporate personnel offices has been that company officials are more conscious of EEO matters. This change is evident in several ways. The yards have expanded their recruiting efforts, especially into minority communities and through newspapers and other media which serve those communities. Screening, testing, placement, transfer, and promotion procedures have been restructured. Cynics might say that these changes have been implemented solely for the purpose of avoiding Title VII litigation; nonetheless, they have occurred.

In addition, these are not temporary, individual changes. Personnel procedures have been reorganized so that EEO officers have access to the entire decision-making process. Monitoring of these changes takes place in two ways: extensive record keeping and the establishment of an accounting mechanism. By the latter is meant that the EEO operation is reviewed by a top manager at each yard; hence, accountability is effected through a reporting mechanism that pinpoints responsibility.

Further, the yards have introduced different kinds of biracial committees (often renamed affirmative action committees in deference to pressure for changes affecting women) to handle EEO grievances inside yard operations. Although conditions may remain less than ideal, the impact of federal efforts has contributed to the creation of a pervasive atmosphere of EEO consciousness.

The Seattle yards have experienced similar changes, but to a lesser degree, influenced by their preoccupation with economic survival.

The Role of Organized Labor

The shipyards under study have three different kinds of unions. The Peninsula Shipbuilders Association in Newport News is an independent union which grew out of one of the original Bethlehem plans. The Alabama Dry Dock Company is organized by Local 18 of the Industrial Union of Marine Shipbuilders of America. The Pascagoula and Seattle yards bargain with a Metal Trades Council.

A number of issues relating to unions and EEO interests have arisen, but the dominant one has been seniority. The conflict between rights earned under a collective bargaining contract and those won under Title VII cases, consent decrees, and negotiated settlements is not unique to shipbuilding, but this industry represents a good laboratory for observation of this conflict and its effects.

There have been a number of responses to a basic situation in the shipyards. The basic situation (common to collective bargaining agreements in other industries) is that seniority is earned in a line of progression or a unit (sometimes called a department). All of these arrangements may be termed unit seniority.

Unit seniority confers advantages to incumbents over outsiders, including access to promotion, opportunity for transfer, protection against layoff, and preference for recall. Where an affected-class settlement is made, it rests on unit seniority clauses in collective agreements and past placements based on minority or nonminority status.

The June 12, 1970, agreement at Newport News called for dual seniority as a remedy. Members of the affected class were allowed to retain their seniority in their old line for a certain period while they gained seniority in the new line. (This dual seniority is common in collective bargaining agreements even where minority status is not a factor.)

However, race was a determinant of initial placement in the Newport News yard up to July 1, 1966; hence the affected class was defined as including those blacks who were placed in certain units prior to July 1966 because of their race. In the settlement, class members were given bidding rights with rate retention to formerly restricted lines. There was no provision for carry-forward seniority.

The agreement in Pascagoula provided for carry-forward seniority: Once members of the affected class won a rating in the new line, they could exercise plantwide seniority. The union, which had resisted this provision originally, settled for a clause which was considered by outsiders to be a "featherbedding" arrangement: that no worker not in the affected class would suffer unemployment or wage reduction as a consequence of rights won by members of the affected class. The company agreed to this clause, knowing that employment would increase by the thousands in the near future.

The demand for carry-forward seniority at the Alabama Dry Dock Company produced a lawsuit. When the OCR presented its proposed package, the union responded that it would accept the provision only if the company would guarantee a clause similar to the one reached in Pascagoula. The company—with no similar assurance of growth—refused.

When the OCR insisted on carry-forward seniority, the company relented but refused to guarantee rights to workers not in the affected class. Consequently, the union filed a breach-of-contract suit. The union's motivation was not to avoid carry-forward seniority but to protect its members from what it perceived to be a threat to jobs—losses which have not, in fact, occurred.

How should the union response be evaluated? The union is duty-bound to defend rights earned for its members over the years, but it is also barred from defending illegal contract provisions. Until the issue was resolved in the courts (see the Crown Zellerbach decision cited in Chapter 1), it was understandable that unions would file breach-of-contract suits where such vital rights as those won in seniority were threatened.

However, unions also have a responsibility to represent their minority members. Thus, the issue of going to court often becomes a political matter. Because the Landrum-Griffin Act mandates that local unions must hold elections at least every three years, the political issue may become the dominant one—along with the percentage of minorities in each local union.

The Fifth Circuit has made it clear that seniority systems may be restructured when unit seniority and discriminatory placement policies combine to produce an affected class, so the extreme response of Local 18 in filing suit could be considered unusual; however, it is probable that the union chose litigation because of the internal political issues involved.

In the Pascagoula case, the unions faced the threat of decertification and thus effected a complete turnaround on their racial policies. At the same time, they bargained for what the company considered (correctly) a face-saving clause involving no additional company expense.

In the Newport News settlement, there was no official union objection—which might be related to the extremely high black percentage in the membership and to the efforts of the union after the Blumrosen agreement in resolving problems concerning racial discrimination. The Seattle situation, however, was quite different.

Alabama, Mississippi, and Virginia all have state right-to-work laws; Washington does not. In addition, the city of Seattle is a strong union town. The Metal Trades Council in Seattle successfully bargained for an agreement giving it the right to fill openings with qualified applicants within the first 48 hours after the announcement of such openings. This has been in effect a closed-shop provision. (Attorneys may disagree about the nuances of the law on this issue, but labor economists usually do not.)

Although the Metal Trades Council was certainly aware of the EEO demands being made on the yards by the subregional office of the Maritime Administration, it had the rights of its members to defend. Since no complaints had been filed and because of the deteriorating economic conditions for Lockheed and the Seattle economy, no attempt was made to negotiate an affected-class settlement at the Lockheed yard. The existing agreement protected union members' rights—rights which had derived in part from past policies of discrimination at the yard. Given the low percentage of minorities in the area and in the Metal Trades Council, it is clear that the union leadership had no particular incentive to take the initiative in changing personnel policies. (It is less clear why the OCR remained inactive, but its strongest defense was probably the absence of complaints.)

The unions have acted predictably. The settlement in Newport News constituted no real threat to the union, especially in light of its posture of avoiding racial problems. There was no dispute in Pascagoula because growth made the issue moot. The affected-class issue has not been raised in Seattle. In the Alabama Dry Dock case, the union proceeded to litigation in response to the direct threat to its raison d'être.

Some have contended that unions are basically political organizations concerned primarily with their survival as institutions. We have discovered no evidence in this study to contradict this view.

The Contribution of Outreach

The outreach concept was developed for a specific industry: contract construction. However, its success in that industry had led to its use in other industries as well, including shipyards. Shipyards do a considerable amount of construction and are often organized by the same unions active in building contracts. We found specific examples of the application of outreach in two areas: Seattle and Pascagoula.

The SOIC operation has been plagued by incredibly poor labor-market conditions. However, it has been able to secure two contracts for 60 welders each. Graduates of these programs were hired at the yards in the lowest welder classifications.

Two different kinds of operations function in Pascagoula in conjunction with the Ingalls yard. The smaller one, the HRDI, concentrates on the disadvantaged, primarily ex-convicts. The larger unit, the RTP, slots young applicants into shipbuilding apprenticeship programs for the skilled crafts in the Metal Trades Council and the IBEW (which is not a member of the Metal Trades Council).

The number of employees involved in these programs is small when compared to the volume of recruitment conducted by the yards (except for the RTP effort in Pascagoula since 1974). No specific involvement by outreach agencies in the personnel efforts of the yards in Mobile and Newport News has been seen.

Data are scarce on outreach operations in shipbuilding, but information from the Pascagoula RTP project indicates significant upgrading for its placements, which included many women and a substantial majority of blacks. The Pascagoula RTP experience suggests that there may be a significant role for outreach organizations in shipbuilding.

Women in Shipbuilding

Executive Order 11246 conspicuously omitted any reference to sex. This omission was corrected by Executive Order 11375 (issued in 1968). In December 1971 the OFCC released Revised Order 4, requiring that goals and timetables for women be established in affirmative action plans. Token breakthroughs have taken place in Newport News, Seattle, and Mobile. The prevalent attitude appears to be grudging acceptance of women in nontraditional jobs as long as they can do the work.

Although tokenism appears to be the rule in many industries beside shipbuilding, the Ingalls yard in Pascagoula demonstrated a significant change in the sex composition of its blue-collar work force between early 1972 and August 1973.

In early 1972 Litton employed 232 women in the craft, operative, and laboring jobs (some 2 percent of the total blue-collar work force). By August 1973 the number of women employed had risen to 918, representing nearly 8 percent of all blue-collar jobs at the yard. In addition, the August 1973 female blue-collar work force was approximately 63 percent black.

Interviews with personnel officials at the yard indicated that the women had better attendance records and less turnover than the men (which may simply be an indication of the relative absence of economic alternatives for females). The major point to be learned, however, is that the World War II experience can be replicated with a minimum of disruption. The major shift in the next five years in the personnel operations of shipyards will probably be an increasing emphasis on placing women in blue-collar jobs.

Benchmarks and Training

Two important issues which arose in the course of this study were: the use of a minority population percentage for an evaluating benchmark for the participation of minorities in the labor force, and the use of shipyards as training institutions.

The equal opportunity officers and the Washington, D.C., staff of the OCR use a benchmark figure based on 1970 census data. Our first reservation about this measure is that the figure used should relate to labor-force participation rather than population.

However, our primary concern is with the rigidity of this measure. It brings to light the twin concerns of enforcement authorities—underrepresentation and concentration. Scholars of fair employment practices are familiar with company profiles indicating that minorities and women are concentrated in some job titles and underrepresented in others. The difficulty in using a benchmark figure as a goal is that it carries with it an implied maximum number of jobs for minorities. When applied to a single establishment, a benchmark figure requires an unrealistic rigidity in personnel policies.

Our plea, therefore, is for a "confidence level" (to use a statistical term) of several percentage points above or below the benchmark. This flexibility would be no more than a recognition of minority and nonminority preferences; even more important, it recognizes the necessity for channeling larger percentages of women and minorities into entry-level jobs in lines of progression to provide the training which they have so long been denied. Nowhere is this more evident than in shipbuilding.

Large shipyards are massive training institutions. Not surprisingly, most of the workers trained are young and inexperienced. Thus shipbuilding performs a socially useful training role, especially for minorities.

Affected-Class Settlements: Problems and Prospects

The heart of the successful cases is in their emphasis on affected-class settlements. However, there has been no apparent numerical relationship between such settlements and changes in the EEO stance of some yards, which raises some interesting points.

First, with the exception of the growth case in Pascagoula, the movement of members of an affected class has often been of an extremely small magnitude. If the affected-class settlements accomplish little by themselves and have no apparent numerical relationship to EEO changes, we might very well ask, why bother?

The simplest issue to resolve is that dealing with the relatively minor movement of workers following an affected-class settlement. All of the unions involved (industrial or trade unions) have bargained for contracts whose monetary provisions result in wage leveling. That is, there is little difference between the wage rates for various lines of work in the shipyards.

In addition, most members of the affected classes have been older than the average shipyard workers; many were in their forties or older. These workers had an understandable reluctance to learn a new trade (although some may have wanted the opportunity specified in writing just because it had been denied for so long).

The kinds of shifts in tasks most workers chose involved moves from extremes of hot or cold to the regulated temperatures of a tool shed or an inside maintenance assignment. But there was rarely any wholesale movement following the posting of a notice announcing the affected-class settlement.

The more difficult question remains, however, of why the yards had to undergo such traumatic negotiations in the first place. The settlements cost time, energy, and money. Apparently this exercise is necessary before yard managements will pledge never again to practice discriminatory personnel policies. Their resolve after settlements is strong.

The civil rights enforcement bureaucracy needs to devise an imaginative solution which will produce the resolve without the trauma of negotiated settlements first. Without that commitment on the part of unions and managements, the initiative will remain with the enforcement authorities. Until corporations and unions restructure their policies to reflect improved EEO practices, the civil rights staff of the government will unfortunately remain fully employed.

A final question might be, if the affected-class settlements themselves have produced very little movement and the yards negotiating them have moved into compliance, then who benefited? The answer generally has been the younger minorities, many of whom were outsiders or short-tenured workers at the time affected-class negotiations began. Hence, the plight of the older minorities has facilitated the movement of younger minorities into better jobs and lines of progression at the yards. Women in blue-collar jobs, all of whom were outsiders only a few years ago, have also been beneficiaries of the EEO gains.

NOTES

1. Lester Rubin, *The Negro in the Shipbuilding Industry* (Philadelphia: University of Pennsylvania, 1970), p. 5.

2. Ibid.

3. Document in files, Center for the Study of Human Resources, University of Texas, Austin.

4. Lester Rubin, *Measures of Effectiveness of the Office of Civil Rights, U.S. Maritime Administration* (Philadelphia: University of Pennsylvania, 1973).

5. Rubin, *The Negro in the Shipbuilding Industry*, op. cit., Chapters II–IV.

6. Herbert R. Northrup, *Organized Labor and the Negro* (New York: Harper and Brothers, 1944), p. 229.

7. Alfred W. Blumrosen, *Black Employment and the Law* (New Brunswick, N.J.: Rutgers University Press, 1970), p. 332.

8. Ibid., pp. 328–407.

9. Rubin, *The Negro in the Shipbuilding Industry*, op. cit.

10. Blumrosen, op. cit., p. 336.

11. Rubin, *The Negro in the Shipbuilding Industry*, op. cit.

12. Ibid.

13. Supplemental Affirmative Action Program for Equal Employment Opportunity at the Newport News Shipbuilding and Dry Dock Company, June 12, 1970, p. 10.

14. Rubin, *The Negro in the Shipbuilding Industry*, op. cit.

15. Interview with an official of the yard, March 30, 1974.

16. Memo filed by an investigator for the Office of Civil Rights, Maritime Administration. Undated but written after August 1972.

17. Ibid.

18. Compliance review filed by staff of the Office of Civil Rights, Maritime Administration, New Orleans, April 12, 1973.

19. Interview with officials of the Metal Trades Council, Pascagoula, Mississippi, August 1974.

20. Interview with personnel official in Pascagoula, Mississippi, August 1974.

21. *United States v. Local 86, International Association of Bridge, Structural, Ornamental and Reinforcing Iron Workers*, 315 F. Supp. 1202 (W.D. Wash. 1970), 443 F.2d 544 (9th Cir. 1971).

22. F. Ray Marshall and Virgil Christian, Jr., eds., *Employment of Blacks in the South: A Perspective on the 1960s* (Austin: University of Texas Press, 1978).

4

SUMMARY AND
CONCLUSIONS

The elimination of institutional discrimination through the courts on a case-by-case basis is expensive, time-consuming, and uncertain in outcome. Victory in court does not assure the elimination of discrimination at the workplace. Some elements of institutional discrimination are outside the control of the individual employer or union.

Moreover, even for matters amenable to change through the courts, the elimination of discrimination, persistent followup, and constant surveillance are necessary to bring about the desired economic changes. Sometimes, as in the Ironworkers Local 86 case, effective followup may be prompted through the vigilance of a minority-based organization. In shipbuilding, the OCR has institutionalized its followup procedure by developing a set of continuing relationships between OCR regional officials and the parties involved at the shipyards.

One major difference between cases which are relatively effective in bringing about equal opportunity and those which are not has been monitoring. Few of the court cases examined in this study made provision for adequate monitoring. The exception was the Ironworkers Local 86 case in Seattle, and even there detailed monitoring procedures were implemented only after demonstrations by an activist black group, the United Construction Workers Association, brought the attention of the judge and the public to the ineffectiveness of the order.

The monitoring expense in the Ironworkers Local 86 case (in terms of time, money, and effort) was perhaps greater than for any individual equal opportunity court case in the construction industry. It includes the continued attention of the judge, who was still issuing supplemental orders on the case six years after his initial order; a part-time special master; a full-time lawyer assigned by the EEOC to monitor the case and to write detailed quarterly reports on progress in the apprenticeship program; the time of the Court Order Advisory

Committee and a full executive staff, funded by the Department of Labor to recruit and support black apprentices; a CETA*-funded operating engineers oiler training program; and, perhaps most important, the continuing surveillance of the UCWA.

Despite all of the monitoring resources mentioned above, progress made toward equal employment opportunity in Seattle has been disappointingly slow and grudgingly conceded by the unions and employers. As Table 2.9 indicated, the goals established in the March 12, 1974, consent decree had not been met almost six and one-half years after the initial court order. In fact, counting all senior apprentices "in the pipe" along with graduates, by September 1976, individual unions affected by the suit had attained only 61.5 to 86.7 percent of their goal.

Why has the progress been so slow? For one thing, the unions did very little to comply immediately with the order, because they felt certain to win an appeal; this delayed progress an additional eight months from the initial decision. Furthermore, the unions and employers involved are not anxious to meet the terms of the decision only to become vulnerable to later suits from nonblack minorities or women or to suits requesting stricter population-based goals and timetables for blacks.

Despite the frustration in achieving equal opportunity in the Ironworkers Local 86 case and other construction suits, much can be learned from the experience. Among the points to be noted by judges, attorneys, and officials of minority-based organizations are the following:

When faced with recalcitrant employers and unions whose racial attitudes may have been stiffened by the filing of litigation, monitoring becomes an enormous and expensive task, especially in a labor market as complex as construction. Perhaps some method could be devised wherein the losing defendant had to bear at least some of the financial burden of the monitoring function, just as the loser pays the court costs in many cases. The monitor would continue to be selected by the court, perhaps with input from the plaintiffs and defendants. Such a plan might have the additional benefit of providing financial incentives to induce defendants to remedy labor-force imbalances as quickly as possible.

Organized minorities play a very important role in enhancing the effectiveness of EEO court decisions in construction. This role includes that of catalyzing action and continuing surveillance as well as that of recruitment and referral. However, maintaining interest and a viable organization throughout the court proceedings and through the implementation of an order without a secure source of funding is difficult, and few minority organizations have this capability.

---

*Comprehensive Employment and Training Act of 1973.

Further, even if money were provided to such organizations, it must be under conditions which would not impair their activist role in facilitating the enforcement of court orders. In contrast to the minorities who were organized to provide input to many construction-industry hometown plans, the minority groups who initiate their own surveillance of court-ordered remedies have a strong interest in and prior knowledge of the construction industry.

Officials of minority organizations interviewed during this study acknowledged that they have learned some important lessons in attempting to integrate construction unions. For example, contrary to their initial impressions, no more than a few black craft workers were found who were willing and able to join building trades unions as fully qualified journeymen. In addition, ignoring qualifications and aptitude in recruitment of apprentices led to unacceptably high dropout rates in the program.

A second major cause of minority apprentice dropouts is lack of work opportunities during apprenticeship. This is evident in EEOC followup reports on the Ironworkers Local 86 case in Seattle. Once a minority apprentice is indentured, efforts must be made to ensure that he or she obtains adequate job referrals and that there is no discrimination between white and minority apprentices in quantity or quality of job referrals offered.

In cases involving construction labor markets with referring unions, it is generally a mistake to leave employers out of the suit and to aim for the unions exclusively, for this leaves the court with the collective bargaining agreement as its only recourse against employer actions. Some leverage is needed over employers; for example, to stimulate them to keep minority apprentices steadily employed.

It is quite useful to establish a forum where minorities, employers, and union officials can meet face-to-face and communicate in working out the problems of integration. Such a forum provides for diffusion of hostility, for education and socialization of all of the parties, and for all parties to have an opportunity to participate in implementing the decree. In this regard, one of the most promising devices has been the Court Order Advisory Committee, such as in the Ironworkers Local 86 case. Chaired by a neutral, this committee might serve as a model for similar cases.

Although worthy in intent, special training programs for blacks parallel to the regular apprenticeship programs have usually proved to be a mistake. Often such programs tend to stigmatize black trainees or provide inferior training which serves them poorly upon graduation. This is especially true in programs where the trainees begin with little or no prior experience or knowledge of the craft. This lesson was clearly demonstrated by the experience in the Ironworkers Local 86 case in Seattle.

CONCLUSIONS ON LEGAL REMEDIES

The direct impact of federal, state, or local civil rights legislation and court decisions on black employment has been limited. In part, the limitations of legal procedure are due to correctable defects such as inadequate funding, a recessionary economy, lack of monitoring followup to litigation, and lack of coordination among government agencies with responsibilities in the area of equal employment opportunity (although some differences among them must be recognized as inevitable because of their different missions, constituencies, and powers).

Yet with all foreseeable improvements, legal procedures are incomplete tools in the fight for equality in employment. For one thing, under the U.S. system, the evolution of the law and legal principles is a slow process. Experience to date suggests that there is little hope of avoiding a case-by-case approach, especially in seniority cases, where different racial histories, technologies, and skill requirements make generalizations difficult.

Legal sanctions, moreover, can do more to strike at overt forms of discrimination than they can to change the patterns permeating social, political, and economic institutions. Hopefully, of course, measures curtailing overt discrimination will also initiate changes in the institutionalized patterns, but by generating conflict, legal approaches also lead to a stiffening of position on racial questions, therefore increasing resistance to change. This was amply illustrated in the Lathers Local 46 case in New York City, cited in Chapter 2.

Legal approaches are also limited because, in the economist's language, they operate only on the demand side of the problem and do little to change supply. Lowering racial barriers does not ensure an adequate supply of qualified people to take advantage of new opportunities. Under Title VII of the Civil Rights Act of 1964, employers and unions can be compelled to stop discriminating against blacks, but they apparently cannot be compelled to recruit, hire, and train them. Positive approaches such as outreach programs are required to provide this training. Affirmative action programs are a tacit recognition of this conclusion and can change supplies where they are established by consent decree or by voluntary programs.

In fact, the threat of the law frequently has more impact than its actual implementation. Courts can achieve much more in a consent decree than they can require of employers in a judicial order. Similarly, compliance officers holding the threat of contract delay or cancellation, or debarment from future contracts, have the leverage to insist upon changes in conciliation with government contractors that could not be obtained by compulsion.

While there is considerable apprehension by employers and unions about the detrimental effects of the civil rights challenge, government agencies seem, in general, to have strained to preserve traditional business practices. Federal courts, however, are demonstrably unwilling to permit subterfuges that perpetuate discrimination under the guise of legitimate business practices. In Seattle, Cincinnati, New Orleans, and other cities, courts have ordered unions and employers to adopt measures to cure racial discrimination through reduction of union ahd employer control of apprenticeship, job referrals, and the determination of standards and qualifications.

Present trends strongly suggest that only determined efforts to establish equal employment opportunity within companies and unions will preserve established procedures from modification by the courts or government agencies. Experience has also demonstrated that those unions and employers which resist equal opportunity changes most are those who will ultimately have to make the greatest adjustments.

CONCLUSIONS ON CONTRACT COMPLIANCE

The case of shipbuilding illustrates that compliance activity can be effective but that many ingredients must come together to make success a reality. One environmental circumstance concurrently enhancing the power of the OCR during this period was the evolutionary development of tighter, more complete, and tougher remedies in racial discrimination cases in the courts.

Although the judicial process has inherent weaknesses as a remedy to discrimination, the evolution of the law in the courts does enhance the bargaining position of compliance agencies which keep abreast of judicial developments and can propose newly ordered court remedies (red-circling, back pay, carry-forward seniority, and so on) during compliance negotiations.

In a natural attempt to close all avenues of escape to discriminators, supplementary and subsequent court orders have placed more detailed and/or severe controls on industry and union personnel procedures (albeit often without adequate knowledge of the industry or sufficient followup). Such orders have proved disruptive and sometimes ineffective, but they nonetheless constitute a threat which can be used to advantage by compliance agencies. The evolutionary character of the judicial process implies that recalcitrant employers and unions who delay settlements are likely to face exposure later to even more dire remedies.

Several other specific environmental factors have also facilitated achievements in shipbuilding. The first has been an active compliance effort on the part of the OCR, operating with the full support of its agency chief.

Second, the fact that government contracts comprise a large portion of the shipbuilding work available provides the OCR with effective leverage through its ability to withhold or delay work or to debar firms from future work. In addition, the structure of the industry is concentrated such that the few major employers are located in limited geographic (coastal) areas, thus facilitating administration and surveillance by a typically understaffed compliance agency.

Third, partly because of the undesirable nature of much of shipbuilding work and because of severe fluctuations in the size of its labor force, the industry has traditionally experienced difficulties in attracting and maintaining workers; this is reflected in extremely high turnover rates. Moreover, at least three of the major yards—Newport News, Ingalls (Litton), and Alabama Dry Dock—are located in labor markets which have been relatively tight during the recent past.

The shipbuilding experience has shown that compliance can work. The success achieved in shipbuilding should not be minimized, and it could not have been achieved without an active compliance effort. Moreover, the industry's success has implications far beyond its own labor force. Because of the high turnover in shipbuilding, it is virtually a training institution offering preparation for entry into a wide variety of skilled occupations, including several construction trades.

Although success in shipbuilding was facilitated by a variety of favorable circumstances, notably lacking was persistent action by organized minorities pressing for reform in the industry. Such organized efforts on the part of minorities in other industries can play a significant role, compensating for the lack of many of the favorable environmental factors present in shipbuilding. We have discovered in our studies of construction industry cases that behind every successful court decision increasing access to employment for minorities has been a persistent and firm effort on the part of a minority organization.

In conclusion, good work on the part of the OCR has demonstrated that compliance can be used effectively to improve the employment status of blacks. Unfortunately, these cases are rare. If compliance agencies can understand their role as that of bargaining to reduce discrimination in a multiactor situation and if they can learn to recognize and act on favorable environmental circumstances, then significant progress can be made in remedying employment discrimination. The key is finding leverage to make it clear to employers and unions that it is in their own interest not to discriminate.

CONCEPTUAL FRAMEWORK: A FINAL STATEMENT

These cases also provide some insight into the basic forces at work causing blacks to have been excluded from jobs and becoming included once sufficient pressures for change are developed.

We have argued that discrimination is based on status plus an economic motive, which varies according to the principal actors—that is, status plus profits for employers and status plus job control for workers. To change racial practices by unions and employers, litigation must threaten some highly valued control mechanism or interest or offer some advantage to employers, workers, and their organizations.

The main instruments of change have been black workers and their organizations, the courts, and various government agencies concerned with industrial relations and equal opportunity matters. These cases indicate that change in minority employment patterns is more likely when the minorities themselves are organized to bring pressure for change and when litigation is accompanied by an outreach effort to recruit, train, and place qualified minorities. These cases also suggest that legal orders without outreach programs are unlikely to be very effective.

These cases suggest the need to gear remedies to labor-market realities. A major reason for the limited success of various "plans" in the construction industry was their failure to attach minority workers to the labor market—having them placed on federal jobs has no long-term effect once those contracts are completed.

Remedies should also be alert to the influence of market and union structure. Only limited change is likely to occur where pressure for change is brought primarily on local union leaders in the building trades, especially where those leaders have strong market-control reasons to resist change. Local leaders are vulnerable politically and are often responsible for only part of the labor market.

On the other hand, national agreements are more effective, because national union leaders are not as vulnerable politically, usually have better staffs to consider the implications of agreement, and are more responsive to pressures for change in unacceptable racial practices. National agreements would therefore be more effective than the local plans promoted by the Department of Labor.

National plans would also make it possible to achieve more effective minority participation. A major problem in the local areas was rivalry between local minority organizations. This would be troublesome at the national level, but there are fewer generally accepted national minority organizations. If participation were restricted to minority organizations with effective outreach capability, the field would be narrowed considerably.

National agreements would also make it possible to develop minimum national qualification standards for various occupations. These standards are necessary in order to resolve disputes regarding when a worker is a qualified journeyman eligible for union membership. Since apprenticeship-trained journeymen are less vulnerable to unemployment, learn the trade faster, and are upgraded to supervisory positions faster, a national objective should be to acquire as many skilled workers as possible through apprenticeship programs.

In addition, since "specialists" are recognized in every craft and whites are often admitted without serving apprenticeships, these specialties should be standardized and minorities admitted on a nondiscriminatory basis as labor market conditions permit. Once admitted, specialist workers should have the opportunity and encouragement to upgrade themselves into fully trained journeymen. It is certainly in the interest of the workers and unions involved to make it possible for specialists to be upgraded into fully capable journeymen.

Of course, unemployment is a major obstacle to improvement of minority employment in both construction and nonconstruction industries. Unemployment not only makes it difficult to upgrade minority employment patterns; it even makes it difficult for minorities to retain the jobs they acquired during the 1960s. Since blacks often have less seniority, they are the most vulnerable to layoffs.

There is the strong temptation to argue for "preferential treatment" and the retention of minorities during periods of high unemployment in order to make it possible for them to preserve some of the hard-won employment gains of the 1960s. However, preferential treatment not only is unfair to whites but threatens the seniority system, which, in the long run, protects the interests of both blacks and whites.

Moreover, preferential treatment of minorities during layoffs will intensify white resistance to change, making it more difficult to achieve negotiated programs enabling blacks to continue their economic progress. Clearly, black *and* white support will be necessary to achieve full employment and racial justice.

With respect to hiring and entry into jobs, we are persuaded that preferential treatment and quotas are unnecessary where outreach programs operate effectively. In other words, it is quite appropriate for government agencies to assign quotas to government-funded agencies to recruit and prepare people to meet minimum qualifications, but it would be inadvisable or unnecessary to require that minorities be accepted who did not meet minimum standards. Where overt discrimination does not exist, outreach programs can make quotas and preferential treatment unnecessary.

However, it is quite appropriate for the courts and other legal agencies to require preferential treatment to correct patterns of discrimination which have been proved after the judicial requirements of due process have been exhausted.

Racial discrimination is based on economic and status considerations. Changing minority employment patterns will, gradually, destroy myths concerning racial superiority and therefore the status reasons for discrimination. Strategies for change must recognize the legitimate economic interests of the parties while eliminating illegitimate practices based on race.

ABOUT THE AUTHORS

RAY MARSHALL is U.S. Secretary of Labor and a nationally recognized economist known for his work on labor market discrimination. A past president of the Industrial Relations Research Association and the Southern Economic Association, his previous books include *The Negro and Apprenticeship*, coauthored with Vernon M. Briggs, Jr., *The Negro Worker, The Negro and Organized Labor*, and *Employment of Blacks in the South: A Perspective on the 1960s*, coedited with Virgil Christian, Jr. Mr. Marshall received his Ph.D. in economics from the University of California at Berkeley.

CHARLES B. KNAPP is a special assistant to the U.S. Secretary of Labor and an economist with interests in the fields of human resources, public finance, and health economics. He has served as a consultant to the Ford Foundation, the Robert Wood Johnson Foundation, and the Rand Corporation and has published articles in several professional journals, including *Economic Inquiry, Industrial and Labor Relations Review, Journal of Political Economy*, and *The Journal of Human Resources.* Mr. Knapp received a Ph.D. in economics from the University of Wisconsin at Madison.

MALCOLM H. LIGGETT is a Staff Economist with the Council on Wage and Price Stability in the Executive Office of the President. Prior to this position, he taught at Cornell University, the University of California at Santa Barbara, California State University, Los Angeles, and San Francisco State University. His articles have appeared in the *Industrial and Labor Relations Review* and in *Proceedings, Industrial Relations Research Association.* Mr. Liggett received a Ph.D. in economics from Cornell University.

ROBERT W. GLOVER is Acting Director of the Center for the Study of Human Resources and Assistant Professor at the Lyndon B. Johnson School of Public Affairs at the University of Texas at Austin. He is also Chairman of the Federal Committee on Apprenticeship. His published work on employment and job training includes *Training and Entry into Union Construction* (coauthored with Ray Marshall and William S. Franklin) and *Minority Enterprise in Construction*. Mr. Glover received his Ph.D. in economics from the University of Texas at Austin.

The work on which this book is based was performed from 1974 through 1976, when all of the authors were affiliated with the Center for the Study of Human Resources.

THE CENTER FOR THE STUDY OF HUMAN RESOURCES, initiated in June 1970 at the University of Texas at Austin, is an interdisciplinary research and training center focused on policy issues concerning education and training, labor markets, equal opportunity, and rural development. Whenever possible, research projects are linked to demonstration efforts to field-test ideas in operating projects.

Key attention is devoted to the following subjects related to human resource development:

Economic policy, particularly economic development of lagging regions and unemployed, underemployed, or subemployed people.

Employment and training programs, including labor-market adjustment procedures, job information and projections, the movement of workers between areas, skill training, preemployment training, and public employment.

Antidiscrimination programs and policies.

Education, with special emphasis on the role of education in the preparation for work.

Health, welfare, and income maintenance, with special emphasis on the use of these activities to support manpower programs.

RELATED TITLES
Published by
Praeger Special Studies

MINORITY ENTERPRISE IN CONSTRUCTION

Robert W. Glover

MINORITY ACCESS TO FEDERAL GRANTS-IN-AID:
The Gap Between Policy and Performance

John Hope II

OCCUPATIONAL CHOICES AND TRAINING NEEDS:
Prospects for the 1980s

Leonard A. Lecht

FEDERAL EQUAL EMPLOYMENT OPPORTUNITY:
Politics and Public Personnel Administration

David H. Rosenbloom